From the Bottom of the Class

Mike Bush

Hereford: 2009

First published in Great Britain in 2009
by Microlab PO Box 238 Hereford HR1 9GA

A CIP catalogue record for this book
is available from the British Library

ISBN 978-0-9563528-0-4

Designed by Microlab and edited by John Jenkins

Colour photography by Keith James

Printed by Print Plus of Hereford

Contents

Dedication

On several occasions I have suffered in the grip of a mental breakdown, rock bottom in terms of despair and self-esteem. Throughout that struggle my recovery was made possible by one person who never lost faith in me: Angela, my wife and constant supporter. It was her courage that enabled me to make a professional success of my life and achieve, what is in most people's eyes, a fortune. The book is dedicated to her and our wonderful children, Colin and Michelle. No man could wish for a better team.

Acknowledgements

I wish to thank my son Colin, my daughter Michelle, my brother David, his wife Cheryl, uncle Rhys and my cousin Judith for their assistance with my quest for information.

I also wish to thank Keith James, John Hewitt and Bob Bowden who all had a direct input in compiling the book.

My thanks too, to the following people:

My London friends Don and Mary, George and Jackie, Alan and Maureen Millar .

Alan Cracknell and Lorraine

Steve Clements

Dave Rhodes and Alison

Air Force pals of the 81st Entry Apprentices RAF Locking, especially John Dallimore, Alan Chiddicks , John Herring and John Birch.

British Telecom colleagues especially Nigel Prosser and Alan Brookes.

Management and staff of ETL Systems.

Preface

Work Without Hope

All Nature seems at work. Slugs leave their lair –
The bees are stirring – birds are on the wing —
And Winter, slumbering in the open air,
Wears on his smiling face a dream of Spring!
And I, the while, the sole unbusy thing,
Nor honey make, nor pair, nor build, nor sing.

Yet well I ken the banks where amaranths blow,
Have traced the fount whence streams of nectar flow.
Bloom, O ye amaranths! Bloom for whom ye may,
For me ye bloom not! Glide, rich streams, away!
With lips unbrighten'd, wreathless brow, I stroll:
And would you learn the spells that drowse my soul?
Work without Hope draws nectar in a sieve,
And Hope without an object cannot live.

Samuel Taylor Coleridge

Foreword

In a moment or two, with the power of my pen and the authority of my signature, the net worth of my estate will rise to £1m and I will become a millionaire!

We were gathered in one of the executive rooms of Harrison Clarke, my solicitor's, based in Deansway in Worcester city. It was June 11th 2003 and I was 64. A multiplicity of solicitors, assistants, accountants and bankers were all in attendance with the sole aim of bringing about the successful sale of my electronics company Enviro Techniques Ltd, generally known as ETL Systems Ltd, to the new owners Ian Hilditch and Dr Esen Bayar.

A stressful morning of negotiations would be concluded by putting my final signature to a large document in a white ring-binder which was laid out before me. Without deliberation I signed, then a phone call or two made by the bankers confirmed that funds had transferred to my account and we all relaxed, shook hands and retired to the annexe, an adjacent room, where a champagne buffet lunch had been prepared. It was all over.

So ended a life-long yearning to become financially independent. I had made it.

It was never all about making money but, in my case, as much to do with my interest in all things radio and electronics and the sheer pleasure of earning my own living and being accountable to no-one except myself.

Discovering, then developing, my, hitherto hidden, creative talent did not happen until later in my life which up to then was severely affected by learning difficulties, set-backs, disappointments, false starts, nervous breakdowns and alcohol.

Chapter 1

The Early Years and Radio

I was born at home in December 1938. Home was a flat in St Owen Street, Hereford, above the flower shop as it now is, which is almost next door to St John's Methodist Church, coming into the world just in time for the start of the Second World War. I wasn't yet one year old when Nazi Germany invaded Poland in early September and subsequently Britain declared war.

My earliest memories are of panic and fear when, as a baby, I was wrapped in sheets and blankets too tightly for my liking and I could not tell anyone about my suffering – only yell. A fear of restrictions and confinement has stayed with me ever since to the point where even today I always sit in an aisle seat at the cinema or theatre.

Before I was two years old my father had joined the navy and served mostly on HMS Nelson, a 33,900 ton battleship, throughout the war. I have few early recollections except that, I remember repeated news bulletins about the Red Army on our "Radio Relay". This was a system of roof-top cables linking and feeding every house on the College Estate, north of the city, where we lived. We could receive the Light Programme and the Home Service audible from a loud-speaker cabinet with a simple selector switch, situated in the front room.

You would expect a youngster to pick up on the Red Army bulletins simply because colours are one of the first things a child learns. Of course, I had no knowledge of the suffering and enduring hardship relating to this, nor the problems brought about by food rationing which had begun in January 1940, which leads me to mention a well-worn piece of card which I recently found among dad's photos. This is the actual on-board menu for the whole of Christmas Day 1940 on dad's ship "the Nelly" as he liked to call it. It is as follows:

BREAKFAST

Mixed Grill
Rolls & Butter   Marmalade

DINNER

Cream of Tomato Soup

Roast Turkey & Stuffing
Cooked Ham
Roast Potatoes   Cabbage

Christmas Pudding with Brandy Sauce
Fresh Fruit   Mixed Nuts

TEA

Christmas Cake
Bread & Butter
Pineapple Chunks

SUPPER

Cold Roast Pork
Cold Tongue
Tomato Sauce
Mince Pies

Biscuits   Cheese   Coffee

The crew were doing very well that day and also written on the menu was a short verse which put everything into perspective.

Here's to our shipmates with Christmas goodwill!
Here's to the tummies we're hoping to fill!
Eat and be satisfied – don't be afraid…,
This is the answer to Hitler's blockade!

By 1940 we had moved to number 6 Queensway on the College Estate, a roomy, semi-detached rented council house on a newly-built estate slightly northeast of Hereford City.

The days and nights during the war years seemed to merge into one. Occasionally I would accompany my mother to the railway station to meet my dad supposedly arriving at a certain time according to his telegram. This was always at night and there were no gas lights turned on in the streets or at the station. In fact, the station was dismal in the extreme even in the daylight, filthy with grime and soot.

On the occasions dad came home it would be from Scotland when his ship was anchored in Scapa Flow. The train would arrive, blacked out and unlit, in swirls of smoke and steam, screeching to a halt at the platform. And we would wait expectantly, it was often late and sometimes there was no dad.

There were some German air-raids usually at night. The siren would wail and my mother would collect me and my elder brother Bryan and we would shelter underneath a giant concrete slab in the pantry next to the kitchen. There we would stay until the all-clear siren sounded.

In the garden of our house was a brick-built local community-aid shelter. There was one in every street, and we also had an Anderson at the end of the garden path. Neither was ever used and later the brick shelter was demolished and a wooden shed constructed on its concrete base. The Anderson was taken over by prolific clumps of mint.

In July 1942 a lone aircraft dropped two huge bombs on the munitions factory at Rotherwas south of Hereford City. The factory was staffed by several thousand women at the time and 22 people were killed.

A young refugee from Kent, Ruth, was staying with us. She was working at Rotherwas at the time of the raid and received a huge thigh injury. My mother's brown paper and vinegar was considered, then the doctor was fetched to the house to attend to her.

During these early years at 6 Queensway, I remember having an intense fear. It concerned the stairs leading to the bedrooms from the front door hallway. At bedtime I was terrified to go up the stairs and saw only an evil entity at the landing top. I couldn't ever climb the steps on my own. There was never a manifestation as such, only my total fear of the landing space with its blank yellow walls lit by a single bulb.

Myra, Bryan (age 9) and me (age 4) taken in 1942

It was usual for young boys, I am not sure about the girls, to have their tonsils removed. I was part of an intake of 12 youngsters into the county hospital. We were all in one ward with taut and tidy made-up beds and a matron with black stockings, dressed in a starched white and blue uniform, definitely in charge.

On the day of the operations we all wore thick, warm, white-coloured woollen outfits with woollen hats and went to the operating theatre in two trolley loads. I was the last one on the last trolley to go in. The anaesthetist's mask was put over my mouth and nose and I was told to breathe deeply. In no time I was seeing vivid images of the early Birds custard container wrapper logo, the one with the chicken silhouettes on a yellow and black chequered background.

I awoke back in the ward with a very sore throat and was then encouraged to eat some jelly which was set aside on my bedside table. Unfortunately the sunshine through the window had melted it while I was away but I had to have it anyway. After a moment or two I was violently sick retching up black bloody vomit. Later that day my uncle Rhys turned up outside my bedside window with our dog Pip who was excitedly wagging his tail as he recognized me. Pip was a smooth-haired black mongrel, a cross between a sheep-dog and a collie, with a white chest, white paws and white pips above the eyes. Seeing both of them was a great encouragement and a great reward after my ordeal.

I was slowly being educated by listening to the BBC and particularly remember Margot Pardoe's Bunkle Butts In a children's tale of spies and intrigue. Each episode was introduced by Elgar's Chanson de Matin a beautiful piece of music which whenever I hear it, transports me back to those secure, almost tranquil days, where I was a small lost soul oblivious to the grown-ups and their concerns with the sometimes-ugly disturbing events and matters of the day.

My first school was Holmer Infants school near Hereford Racecourse and was next door to the next in line – the senior "proper" school. That was about one and a half miles from our house and for the next five years I walked the distance four times each school day whatever the weather. You couldn't, or wouldn't dare not turn up for school because everyone knew about the awesome powers of Mr Critch; George Critch, the City truant officer and child-catcher.

I went to school for the first time when I was five years old. The morning of the first day was spent with a few others in a sand pit and in the afternoon I was given a pile of wood off-cuts, a bag of nails, and a hammer and told to make a Spitfire.

About a year later (1944) my mother started to receive parcels from America containing sweets – a scarce and mostly unheard of indulgence. These came from dad who was free and easy in New York while HMS Nelson was being given a refit. The shipmates helped each other with the parcels by forwarding them on when they next found themselves in England. British sailors were feted and shown a good time in the Big Apple then and dad, among many other engagements, was introduced to the Andrew Sisters. For years afterwards he would often sing his favourite tune Don't Fence Me In, no doubt thinking of the good times he had had in NY.

Like some of the other British sailors with time on their hands, dad took casual employment in the despatch department of the chain store Sears Roebuck & Co and earned some extra cash. The sweet parcels kept coming but suddenly one day a parcel arrived which had only cigarettes inside the sweet cartons, a much restricted and controlled commodity at that time. This was the forerunner of subsequent parcels containing smuggled contraband much to my mother's dismay and disappointment for she had a sweet tooth.

There were toys, too. I had an airport which consisted of a mapped-out aerodrome printed in colour on a large thick sheet of paper with creases so that it could be folded away. It had wooden aircraft and aircraft hangers and motor vehicles (jeeps) all finished in drab olive green with a white American star on the engine bonnet. I also had a cowboy suit. Bryan, who was five years older than me, had a lovely two-part polished wooden box containing a 3-D binocular viewer and a large set of discs. These

discs carried a matrix of colour photo transparencies. You would slip a disc into a slot in the centre of viewer and then press a trigger button to step between views taken from all over the USA, all in perfect colour and in 3-D!

While in New York dad met Sam Horsfield. He was something to do with the New York gas and electric utilities and pretty high up.

Dad in New York during the war whilst HMS Nelson underwent a refit.

For a long time after the war he would on occasions send food parcels to us.

The food parcels consisted of ham, butter, corned beef, condensed milk, fruit (mostly all tinned) and bars of chocolate. There was a great deal of cheese both processed and sliced, the latter packed in cellophane overprinted with the stars and stripes of the American flag. These occasional food parcels were most welcome since food rationing was still in force and didn't completely end until 1954.

Many years later "Uncle Sam" visited us in Hereford. One evening dad took us all to the Green Man in Fownhope for an evening meal. Eating out was unusual at this time but we all had a wonderful dinner to the accompaniment of Ronnie Joins and his Hawaiian guitars.

Before he left us, Uncle Sam asked me what I would like from America as a gift. I was already into amateur radio by this time, and I asked him if I could have a Vibroplex semi-automatic morse key (also known as a bug key) which generated the dots but not the dashes which the user would form himself by manipulating the paddle which moved to the left and right. In due course a chrome and gold presentation model with jewelled movement arrived and I was beside myself with joy. But, more of all this later.

Sam was to die tragically in a car accident.

After I had transferred from the infants to the upper school next door I soon learned that I was not very bright. My reading and ability to do sums was hopeless, so much so that I could only admire the other pupils in the class who seemed to assimilate everything they were given to learn. Not only did the words have little meaning for me but I had great difficulty absorbing anything.

At first we had to use pencils and then graduate to pen and ink. The little white ink wells were set two to a desk and contained blue ink which was made from powder and water. They always smelled of urine. One day we were in the playground when a never ending US Army convoy motored by on their way to the south coast to embark for Europe. We all cheered and chanted "got any gum chum" aimed at the lorries with the GIs sat in the back. They all stood up and waved and hailed to us and hurled packets of the stuff into the playground. I loved the Americans, their high spirits and generosity.

In the classroom I had some learning successes. We had to learn the multiplication tables up to twelve and we were all tested repeatedly. I got as far as five times, more or less, but only because the learning was by rote, a system of repetition by the whole class chanting for hours each combination loudly in unison with a natural cadence starting at the beginning through to the finish.

On one occasion I turned up at school with a cold and sore throat which my mother had sought to relieve by getting me to inhale the strong fumes of eucalyptus oil. She had sent me off to school with my handkerchief soaked in the stuff. The teacher, Hilda Meeks, ranted and raved at me and my mother, indeed all mothers, for daring to send their offspring to her class and subjecting her to the enforced discomfort of breathing eucalyptus all day long.

We played football at playtime and often the ball would end up in the infants' yard. The two buildings were separated by a rusting iron railing fence about five feet high with a row of exposed sharp pointed nine-inch long spikes across the top. Even so it was usual for someone to climb over the fence and retrieve the ball but it was really an accident just waiting to happen. In due course, it did. My pal

Mark Wright slipped when half way over and his full weight, which was not inconsiderable, bore him down onto the spikes and he became impaled through the stomach. He was rushed to hospital and after lengthy treatment, which lasted six months, he re-emerged at school highly respected and untouchable.

The only means of heating each classroom was by individual large coke-burning cast iron stoves. Our stove was about the size and height of three large beer barrels placed on end and I felt sure it was big enough to power a good size steam-roller. It was fixed at the front of the class benefiting only those fortunate to be sitting in the front half of the room. At lunchtime one cold winter's day it was my turn, together with a fellow classmate called Brian Morris, to replenish the stove with buckets of coke from the stockpile in the yard while everyone else was outside. We opened the access lid at the top of the stove and filled it up to the top as quickly as possible. When the bell rang at the end of the dinner break we all returned to the classroom to find the stove glowing like a furnace, cherry-red at the bottom to white hot at the top, It was so hot that the varnish on the front desks bubbled merrily. Desks and pupils were moved to the back half of the class for the rest of the day. Brian and I went to see the headmaster and received a reprimand, but there was no punishment that I can recall.

January, February and March in 1947 was an arctic white-out with temperatures as low as -15° much of the time. One morning we opened the back door to find a wall of snow higher than the porch roof top. In fact it had drifted up to the bedroom window sills on the first floor. I have no recollection of feeling cold but everyone was cut off and how we ever managed to get food to eat and coal to burn I will never know. I was nine years old at the time.

Our road Queensway is steep and we lived at the bottom. There were few motor vehicles to be seen and the milk was still delivered by horse and two-wheeled cart every morning by Mr Gladwin. The milk was ladled out into a jug or jugs which we had to take to the cart. This meant that if we missed Mr Gladwin then we had no milk. His powerful horse moved the cart without any effort stopping frequently as it progressed up the hill knowing exactly where it was expected to stop on the way.

There was always someone looking out for the horse manure hoping to collect it for the garden.

We played football safely in the street always in organised teams with the winning side nearly always the one with the slope of the hill going for it. The games moved up and down the road whenever we were told to move off by the ladies of the adjacent houses who always appeared at the front gate as if by magic and who always appeared to own, and regard as sacrosanct, the road space outside their dwelling.

Our house, being at the bottom of the hill, gave a good view of everyone's back garden looking upwards from our own. Our immediate neighbours kept chickens but we always filled our garden with vegetables, particularly cauliflowers, cabbages, Brussel sprouts, carrots and potatoes. We saved the peelings from these and took them to Mrs Map who lived further up the road and exchanged them for an egg or two. My favourite food dish of the day was either mother's rabbit pie or boiled cod. The latter was regarded as a poor man's food because it was cheap. But there was nothing better tasting than the large white medallions of loin of cod with fresh parsley sauce, mashed potatoes and peas. These and similar hot dishes were always waiting at lunchtime when I arrived home from school.

The view of the back gardens all the way up the hill was particularly spectacular on November 5 each year, when it seemed that everyone celebrated with mammoth bonfires and displays of fireworks, even if it was damp or wet outside. The estate had many mature roadside trees and we used to sweep up the fallen leaves for the bonfire, much to the delight of the council roadmen, and collect as much general rubbish for the purpose as we possibly could.

The fireworks of the day were vicious. A four-inch banger called Cannon, for example, could be buried a few inches or so in the ground and when lit with an experimental remote fuse, could be expected to blow out a small crater. There were instances of terrible injuries and one friend was rushed to hospital after a so called "Jacky Jumper", a Chinese cracker, shot up his coat sleeve. He was badly burned and had to have many skin grafts. These fireworks were powerful and dangerous things.

My dad had served in HMS Nelson for most of the war during which the ship patrolled the north Atlantic, and sailed as convoy escort going to South Africa and Malta. At the end of the war he rejoined

George Masons grocery store. His pre-war employment with the company had stood him in good stead. Later he was promoted and went to manage The Ross-on-Wye store and then the Monmouth store before setting up his own take-away fish and chip business where I had to help out.

George Masons was in the middle of Hereford High-Town. It was a traditional shop with individual counters for cheese, butter, bacon, sugar, jams and other staples. A sign attached to the bacon slicing machine read:

> "Please do not let your children sit on this counter as we can get a little behind in our orders".

When all of the shopping was gathered a handwritten "bill of sale" itemising everything was completed and put together with payment into a cylinder. The cylinder was then attached to a catapult system which when the actuator (rather like a lavatory chain) was pulled, shot the cylinder at great speed off across the ceiling to the office set high at the back of the shop where the contents were dealt with in turn and change with receipt despatched back in the same manner. All very thorough but it meant a lot of waiting around.

While dad was working at George Masons we were able to take a holiday. This wouldn't be so easy when he started working for himself. For three consecutive years we went to Weymouth and stayed for a week half-board at Mrs Smith's whose house was on the north side of the resort. My first acknowledgement of the opposite sex happened on the last of these Weymouth outings. We all went to see a show at the Pavilion Theatre on the pier and one of the acts consisted of a beautiful young lady roller skating solo to the Barcarole from Offenbach's Tales of Hoffmann. The memory stayed with me for years.

I wasn't to know it at the time but my attraction to the kitchen wireless in the house was the beginning of my life-time interest in all things to do with radio communication. Although we had Radio Relay which gave us the Home Service and the Light Programme, this was different. This set was connected to the mains electricity and was tuneable to all of the exotic continental radio stations on the long and medium wave, each station printed in black on an illuminated mellow yellow dial: stations such as Hilversum, Hamburg, Munich, Luxembourg, Brussels and so on.

Looking into the rear of the wireless set, through the ventilation grill, I was deeply drawn to, and intrigued by, the rounded shiny shapes of the valves with a miniature red illumination deep inside each one. This warm, dark futuristic-looking assembly of components, partly covered in clinging dust, was silently linking our kitchen to the outside world and was simply thrilling to my senses.

For Christmas 1948 my brother received a crystal set. It was a kit of parts which had to be assembled. It was quite easy really. There was a base board with a printed outline of the components and holes drilled to take the screws and parts. It was soon up and running with the earphones, which were part of the kit, connected to it as well as a makeshift aerial and earth. Adjustment of the sharp pointed end of the cat's whisker, a small coil of springy copper, onto the galena crystal in just the right place did the trick and rotating the condenser tuner brought in a station or two on the medium wave during the day and a lot more as dusk developed, all bunched up together at one end of the tuning dial.

It was only some 10 or 15 years earlier, when wireless broadcasting was still developing, that crystal sets were fashionable. They needed no batteries as the signal powered the earphone on its own. My parents and, it seemed, all grown-ups were still quite knowledgeable about this form of radio reception.

Eventually my brother lost interest in his crystal set and it was passed down to me for analysis. My first task was to take it apart. I hadn't a clue how it worked or what I was doing, but taking it apart seemed like the correct thing to do. This emerging clinical destructive power of mine stayed with me for some time to come with all of its wanton devastation-some would say, of precious early radio sets which later, one by one, came into my hands.

These were 1920s valve TRF sets with silver coloured tuning dials, calibrated in degrees, mounted on the front of the cases made from shiny black sheets on the outside and dull black sheets on the inside, of an early material called Ebonite made by processing rubber. A TRF set (tuned radio frequency) was the forerunner of the sensitive superhetrodyne type of wireless, a technique which is still very much in use today.

At this time there existed in Hereford a shop called Stones Radio next door to the Odeon cinema in High-Town. They used to sell, among all things electrical, radio aerial wire, egg insulators and "high tension" and "grid bias" batteries as well as recharging the low voltage "lead acid accumulators" for the many battery radios which were still around. All of these radios would be connected to the batteries by coloured banana plugs except the accumulators which supplied much heavier current to the "heaters" of the wireless valves and were usually connected by large crocodile clips on the end of cables, one red clip for the plus pole and one black for the negative pole of the accumulator.

One day I spotted in Stones shop window a white coloured crystal set shaped like a miniature radio receiver. It measured five and a half inches by three and a half inches and was just three inches deep and was made by Ivelek. I just had to have it.

With this crystal set safely in my custody, there was only one available at the shop, I proceeded to my bedroom to test it. My bedroom window sill became my work bench and from the window my copper wire aerial, some 35 feet long, stretched down to the back of the garden fence. I tended to use the cast iron rain guttering which ran along the house eves just accessible outside the window for my earth connection.

It worked fine but no different to my brother's crystal set before it was disassembled. Soon I had all of the parts before me on the window sill and had discarded the small white case which had protected everything. Earphones and external wires were all connected up and using all of my knowledge, which amounted to nothing, I set about improving reception.

One by one the parts were removed and put to one side. Incredibly I was receiving the Light Programme and the Home Service together and both became louder and louder as I successively removed each component crystal and all. Finally, totally confused, I was left with only the earphones connected to the aerial and the guttering outside, still receiving the broadcasts loud and clear, with the crystal set totally in pieces and discarded!

I have already mentioned the Radio Relay which at that time linked all of the houses together by cable. The cable ran under the eve of my house adjacent to the guttering which I used as an earth and I can now postulate that by means of induction and possible rectification by decaying metal screws holding the metal guttering together, my earphones were doing what they were designed to do and responding to the audio signals which were curiously present. It was possible to listen to either one or the other of the two stations because they were at different volume levels and the ear, at least my ear, was selective. Anyhow from then on I could listen to Radio Relay in bed under the sheets for nothing. The crystal set? Well, that was already history.

Using some of the parts, mainly earphones, I had collected I made a simple telephone system which linked several of my next door friends together, The wire which I bought from Woolworths was known as bell flex and cost me tuppence a yard. We would talk together, as if on a party line, from the secrecy and comfort of our bedrooms. We weren't doing any harm to anyone but it didn't stop one of the neighbour's halting everything by cutting the circuit as it passed across his property.

After the war, surplus radio equipment became available and I acquired an R1224A communications receiver which covered the medium waves and the short waves, the latter being of most interest to me. It was produced by Ferguson in 1942 as a portable battery set for use in forward airfield situations together with the sister transmitter T1442. The receiver case was wooden except for the front panel which was made from sheet metal, the livery was air-force grey. To possess this most desirable wireless I had to hand over money which I had earned by helping in my dad's fish and chip shop.

The chip potato varieties in use at the shop were either King Edward's, Maris Piper, Pentlands or Pembrokes. The preparation process involved peeling them automatically in a centrifuge and afterwards taking out the remaining "eyes" using the tip of a hand peeler. My two widower grandfathers, William and Elijah, used to do this every day with dad always checking that everything was perfect. The grandfathers shared a bedroom at the house at the time and both were World War One veterans. Bill liked to drink beer a lot, dig and look after the garden, and smoke his pipe. Elijah, my dad's father, liked to take ladies to the cinema and to play snooker.

I earned the money for my wireless by helping with the chipping. This consisted of placing the potatoes one at a time, on a matrix of cutter blades and then bringing down the handle to force the spud through. I did buckets and buckets of these. It was not possible to chip too many in advance otherwise they would go brown so I had to be on hand many evenings to perform the operation the moment they were required for the boiling fat in the fryer.

My 1224A allowed me to listen to all of the strange signals on the shortwave frequencies. I couldn't read Morse code yet but there was plenty of that which was sometimes sent fast with some stations slowly repeating their station call sign over and over again thus giving me a chance to identify the individual letters or numbers, then, suddenly, the slow Morse would burst into a fast teletype message which only the distant corresponding receiving machine would be able to read.

This radio gave me insight into the world of amateur radio and the more I learned about it, the more I wanted to participate. Every Sunday morning on the 40 metre band the local radio amateurs would join a so called "net" and I would tune in and although I could only listen and not transmit, I nevertheless felt very much a part of it. One of the loudest signals I ever heard was from a local amateur station G3ESY operated by Peter Jones. I managed to get an invitation to visit him one evening at his house in Holme Lacy road. Peter's wife showed me to his operating room which turned out to be a spare bedroom upstairs and then she disappeared. It was full of radio equipment of all kinds – I was totally agog.

He greeted me and motioned me to sit down on a nearby chair pursing his lips and finger to tell me to be quiet for a moment as he was in voice conversation with a far off station. After listening to

Peter Jones. Radio station G3ESY

the station for a while he turned on his transmitter to respond. The receiver on the table went quiet, the floor standing transmitter made a firm humming sound, the lights dimmed slightly and Peter spoke into the microphone with the accompaniment of a loud "tick" from the wall clock in the background. The far off station was Bill, call sign 5A4TY, who was an American located at Wheelus USAF base near Tripoli in Libya and when it was Bill's turn to speak again, there he was loud and clear greeting me!

Wheelus USAF base existed until 1970 by which time Colonel Gaddaffi had deposed muslim King

Idris who left to settle in Egypt leaving Libya awash with oil. Tripoli was to feature in my life twice more in the future, once incidental and once in a more profound way.

After the war Peter, along with other skilled radio amateurs, was associated with "Y Service" one of the listening arms associated with GCHQ (Government Communications Head Quarters) based in Cheltenham. They were given prime communication receivers such as HRO's and RCA AR88's with which to monitor certain frequencies at certain times on the lookout for clandestine transmissions – presumably Russian.

We were the first family in the road to have a television. This was a Kolster Brands floor model, an upright piece of furniture with a light yellow-grey screen held in a cream coloured plastic border shoe - a baleful looking thing when it wasn't on. Anyone could see we had a "telly" because ours was the only house with a TV H aerial mounted on the chimney. Our neighbours were often invited to the house to see the "box".

One frequent visitor was our vicar, Father Mason. He often came in the afternoon principally to check that I would be attending church on the following Sunday. Our church was St Barnabas in Barrs Court Road and being in the choir I would often turn up for Mass and Evensong and Sunday school. He would always stay for a cup of tea and we would turn on the TV especially for him.

It was 1949 and the 11-plus scholarship tests were nearly upon me. I was moved from my desk well in advance and told to sit next to the class egg-head who I greatly admired – he was invincible. The idea was that he would help me with exercises which we were being given in preparation. It was not fair on him but I guess he wasn't bothered too much as eventually he not only passed the 11-plus but also the entrance exam for the prestigious Cathedral School where, of course, he chose to go. I am sure that if his parents had known about the set up between us they would have had something to say about it. Anyway, as I look back over many years, I owe him a big "thank you" for trying to help me.

FROM THE BOTTOM OF THE CLASS

Chapter 2

High School and Radio

One of the greatest mysteries of 1949 was how I passed the 11-plus examination for entry to Hereford High School for Boys. Holmer, my junior school, was next to Hereford race course where no doubt a punter might have got odds of 100-1 if my prospects had been written up on a bookie's board, if they were remotely interested.

To account for my success there are three possibilities I can think of: The first was that since some of the exam questions were the multi-answer types, I had unwittingly ticked the correct boxes.

Secondly, as I was the son of a businessman, some deference was given to my case. Thirdly, the examiner was simply having a bad day.

Some people say that school years are the best years of one's life. Well they weren't for me. For the next five years I endured endless hours of personal tension in the classroom wondering how I was going to make it to the end of the session. Time and the slow tick-tock of the wall clock were my enemies. In addition to this I had to endure the humiliation of regularly achieving bottom-of-the-class status.

Initiation rites inflicted on new students on their first day were well known. These involved having your head pushed under water during break time by the senior boys and, for some days prior to my arrival, I became anxious about it.

On the day, during morning break, I was grabbed by two seniors and frog-marched to the toilets for the event. The hand basins were full and there was water everywhere and my new shirt and blazer were soaked. The seniors had a production line going and I was caught a second time but after that they left me alone and I was greatly relieved.

My reward for passing the exam was a new Raleigh bicycle, complete with a Sturmey-Archer gear changer fitted to the handle bar. In addition I had a new set of school clothes with two pairs of "whites" consisting of trousers, shirt, jersey and plimsoles for cricket and boots for rugby. Football wasn't played.

During school days it was obligatory to wear the school blazer, tie and cap to and from school, and when in town after school hours.

My generation was among the first to benefit from the 1944 Butler Education Act which made grammar school education open to children from ordinary families. Hitherto such schools were only open to fee-paying pupils.

The system, readily employed and expanded by Attlee's Labour government, produced many leaders in commerce, the arts, armed forces and even politics but for the past generation or so it has been attacked as divisive and unfair.

There is little doubt, however, that it was an improvement on the previous system.

The pupils were organised into Houses, with historical Herefordshire family names, as a vehicle for competitive endeavours. These were DeLacy, Mortimer and Conningsby which I belonged to. Competitions were held in all of the sports, including swimming, and academic achievements. I wasn't a team player but I always turned up at the sports events and cheered, particularly swimming where some of my mates were in with good chances of success.

The masters all wore black gowns and would don their mortar boards for special occasions such as class and school photographs. They would all have to be present at assembly at 9am every school day and they had weird nick-names such as Cager, Smiler, Pop and Tiger.

I hated assembly, I didn't like being hemmed in by a few hundred other people which caused me to sweat and palpitate. Each morning at the close of proceedings we all chanted this dedicated prayer.......

> *O Lord God who art the author and giver of all*
> *good things*
> *Graft in our hearts the love of the name*
> *Keep within us true religion*
> *Nourish us with all goodness*
> *And with thy great mercy*
> *Keep us in the ways of thy life*
> *Now and for ever more*
>
> *Amen*

I eventually memorised it and it served me well on occasions in years to come.

On October 29 1949 my brother David was born at home at 6 Queensway. The next day was my mother's birthday and she was thirty-seven years

David (age 6)
taken in 1955.

old. I remember sitting by the fire in the kitchen in the afternoon unable to make sense of my feelings while the midwives and others were hurriedly making their way through the lounge on their way to the staircase and my mother's bedroom.

In 1951 dad took me to London to the Festival of Britain which was sited beside the river Thames on the South Bank near Waterloo Station. The Festival was a national event celebrating the centenary of the 1861 Exhibition and also, in the words of Labour Deputy Leader Lord Morrison "a tonic to the nation." It was certainly that following the effects of 1939-45 and post-war austerity and rationing.

Even so, there were critics who attacked the expenditure of £8million which could have been spent on much-needed housing. Yet the event was a huge success and the sums involved miniscule when set against the cost of today's Dome and forthcoming Olympics.

As well as the Dome of Discovery and the Royal Festival Hall another exhibit was the Skylon, a tall cigar-shaped metal structure pointing up into the air with little obvious means of support. It was spectacular and I had had a preview because it was assembled and tested for stability at Painter Brothers, a local company, prior to being dismantled and shipped to the Festival site. The Skylon's enormous shape would catch the eye of anyone walking across College Green at the top of the College Estate at that time.

Dad also took me to the Pleasure Gardens at Battersea Park with its Tree Walk, a pathway suspended by chains high among the trees, and also to Hyde Park where we parted company when I was sent for a couple of ice-creams and became lost. A copper took charge of me and we were eventually re-united by which time the ice-creams had completely melted.

While in London we stayed at my uncle's house with his wife Olive and my two cousins Derek and Maureen in Harbiton Road near Archway. His brother's name was Trevor and he was a teacher at a boys' school in Highgate where he was destined to become headmaster. I didn't like him very much and I am sure the feeling was mutual, a stand-off that lasted a lifetime.

We travelled to the exhibition site on one of the few remaining electric trams still in operation. It left Archway and went directly towards the South Bank using the Kingsway Tram Subway. The tram was a double-decker, coloured signal red with cream trim and had dusty smudged windows. Inside there were worn shiny wooden seats and framed faded yellow adverts. The mechanical parts squealed and clanked as it ground its way along the road. Electric trolley buses, probably the cleanest and quietest mode of transport London has ever had, had all but taken over from the tram.

Archway was to figure very much in my life in years to come.

At school there were many new subjects. I marvelled at the mechanics of geometry and algebra when they were introduced to the class for the first time and I had grand notions of becoming a class expert. However, this desire was short-lived because of the inability of my brain to retain any detail, a necessary condition to solving problems in class and when doing homework. As with all subjects, the teacher's words can be likened to a sparrow and my brain likened to a feeding table – the sparrow flies in, stops for a second, and flies off again into thin air!

I was also beginning to have problems putting names to faces of people outside my immediate circle and could not be spontaneous in greeting them. This caused me to feel shy and withdrawn.

To discipline pupils when they performed poorly there were beatings on the hands and bottom with a few hours' detention most evenings after school. I experienced this treatment first hand.

There were school trips and the odd day out at the cinema. The latter was to see the film Scott of the Antarctic at the Ritz, in Commercial Road. I think all the children in Hereford were taken to the special free afternoon showing of the film.

Two trips I paid for were to the Lake District and North Wales. These were both week-long walking and trekking holidays which took place during the summer. In both cases we were a group of about 30 boys looked after by a schoolmaster who usually brought his wife along, too. We travelled by coach and stayed full-board at lodges close to the mountains. In the coach I joined in with the lads who took up the four or so rows of rear seats from where all of the singing came from. We sang Ten Green Bottles, Frankie and Johnny and The Battle Hymn of the Republic with our own words. There were no song books.

Each morning we collected our packed lunches and set off along planned routes and returned to the lodge between four and five o'clock. Weather conditions on the mountains can change suddenly and without warning. One day in the Lake District we were high up walking single-file along the grassy Dodds ridge. The weather was fine but in the valley on our left hundreds of feet below we could see dense black clouds gathering. The clouds swept up the side of the ridge at great speed and enveloped us in swirling sleet. The temperature and visibility dropped dramatically towards zero which forced us to place our hands on the person in front as we shuffled precariously forward in single file. We couldn't protect our faces which were blue with cold but after 20 minutes the storm passed over and we were in the clear again, thankfully.

The High School sports field was next to the Rowing Club on the River Wye and it had a pavilion complete with changing rooms, showers and a small kitchen. The school also had a well-fitted gymnasium with wall bars on each side of the room and two sets of thick ropes suspended from the tall ceiling. Work-outs in the gym made use of all of the apparatus with exercises which included climbing to the top of the ropes. Another exercise was called pirates, a form of tag whereby one team chased another team scrambling over all of the apparatus purposely laid out.

On the sports field, I didn't excel at cricket or rugby but I was chosen to play hooker, a central position in the rugby scrum, on several occasions during house tournaments. During a game we would call for the rugby ball and shout "pass the pill!" as we moved forward. "Pill" would mean something quite different in later years. There was always cross-country running during the sports afternoon and I enjoyed this immensely. Although never coming home in the first three, I set myself the task of never stopping to walk or linger so that I might claim personal satisfaction and sometimes a "well done Bush" at the end.

One year, on the last school day before the summer break, we all went to the House swimming contests at the baths in Edgar Street. Conningsby came top and my friend James McIvor on behalf of the House, collected the trophy which was a large engraved silver cup: quite magnificent with the details of previous winners neatly engraved on the side of it. In the afternoon we went to the sports field for the athletics events. There was a group of us, including James, sitting on the grass some way apart from the events generally fooling about. I, in my wisdom, gave his satchel an almighty kick and my boot made contact with something metallic. There was consternation as James undid his satchel straps and took out the trophy cup which was severely dented and twisted out of shape. With great anxiety, I took charge of the trophy and immediately took it to Oswin's the silversmiths in Broad Street. I think they contacted the school who then paid the bill because I didn't hear anything more about it, thankfully.

It was a pity that in 1976 the school sports fields were sold off and the boys and girls high schools amalgamated to form the Aylestone school.

The school had well-equipped classrooms for chemistry and physics both of which fascinated me but I couldn't profit from the teaching. Chemical valencies and such things went over my head. One afternoon, in the physics lab, we were shown how to make explosive gunpowder by the maths teacher, George Maypole, standing in for the physics teacher "Frowner". Standing behind a raised bench at the front of the class he measured a quantity of saltpetre (potassium nitrate), sulphur and carbon into a mortar and proceeded to grind and combine the mix using the pestle. He then put a small amount of the mixture into the little cup on the end of a deflagrating spoon. This spoon has a long stem-like handle with a circular shield to protect the hand holding it. At the other end of the bench was a Bunsen burner. He took the spoon and its "charge" across to the flame to ignite it and proceeded to demonstrate to the class how pretty the sparks were as they showered all over the place. Unfortunately one spark fell into the mortar detonating the remainder of the gunpowder and producing an almighty explosion which splintered the dish and blasted the pieces in all directions. Everyone in the class ducked for dear life but fortunately no-one was hurt.

For a few seconds after the explosion there was a stunned silence. George Maypole's face had turned white with fear. He asked everyone if they were OK and then left in haste with his black gown in turmoil, to fetch the headmaster who turned up no doubt expecting to see battlefield casualties. No health and safety procedures in these days!

Unaccountably I made a little progress in French, possibly because we spent time learning verbs by rote. The first was the verb être (to be) ; je suis, tu es, il est, elle est, nous sommes, etc. All of these verbs stayed with me and were of great use many years later when I found myself in Paris. The French master "Smiler" was one of the teachers who would call an errant student to the front of the class for a beating. He used a large piece of wood and whacked the pupil across the backside. At the end of term, when there were a few hours with no work to do "Smiler" would tell us about his hobby which was an interest in ancient weapons such as crossbows and flintlock pistols. He would enthral us by showing and demonstrating replica devices he had made himself. Although he loaded a cross-bow with its projectile (known as the bolt), he showed restraint and never fired it. Had he done so, I am sure it would have passed straight through the wall.

I found attempting to learn French much better than attempting to learn English. Often in the English class I was expected to read and comment upon various Shakespeare works but the only one I really remember was Macbeth. This was only because the English master, Mr Woods, organised the play to be performed one evening after school with an invited audience. He arranged for his two daughters who were at the Hereford High School for Girls, across the road from the boys school, to be available to play the parts of Lady Macbeth and Hecate, queen of the witches. Me and some of my pals from the lower ranks were selected to play Birnam Woods and would have to come on stage as soldiers in camouflage when the woods were seen to be on the move in the play.

For our chain mail we used heavy sacking painted in grey and we made swords in the woodwork classroom. With make-up we looked quite the part. However, on the night during the first half of the play "Birnam Woods", swords and all, went down to the White Lion which used to be in Maylord Street and subdued stage fright with pints of cider. We were back in time for our only appearance in the play, in the second half, but only just. In our play, Birnam Woods scene was a spectacle of over-acting due to the need for a toilet and the prospect of returning to the White Lion when the play had ended.

I had already formed a liking for drink at the age of 15, whether it was beer or cider. I used to go to the Rose Gardens Pub in Munstone, north of the city, for a Flowers Poachers, hoping to see Dorothy, the Landlord's attractive daughter, I had known her at Holmer school but I never did see her on these occasions. As senior boys at the High School we would often meet at the City Arms in Broad Street on Saturday evenings and then go to the Chinese Restaurant opposite for a meal. This restaurant, unique to Hereford, was raided frequently by the council food standards officers who were very suspicious.

On the outside wall of the City Arms is a plaque which records that it was a town house belonging to the Duke of Norfolk and that Nelson stayed there in 1802. Across the road is the 15th century Green Dragon Hotel which, as I remember, was the place to be to celebrate New Year's Eve with a throng of people filling the dance floor and bars, and spilling out into Broad Street, partying until the early hours.

At Christmas time the general post office always approached the High School for helpers to assist in delivering the mail during the holidays in the run up to Christmas Day. I needed the money for my radio projects, and for my emerging taste for other things liquid, so one year I volunteered and was accepted.

The mail was sorted at the office opposite the railway station and the helpers would be driven in vans together with the large bags of mail to dropping-off points all over Hereford City. I was dropped off with two huge bags, one across each shoulder, in High Town for I was to service the whole length of Widemarsh Street. My first stop was the chemist shop next door to the Midland Bank. My slight frame weighted down, I stopped outside the shop window and proceeded to untie the first of the many bundles in my bags. I tugged at the string and fumbled in doing so.

In the next second the bundle freed itself from the string and my hands, and the whole lot cascaded through the grill beneath my feet and into the shop cellar below. Much alarmed, I struggled through the shop doorway, with my bags, to ask for assistance to retrieve the letters which had been entrusted to me.

Leaving the bags in the shop I went down to the cellar with a shop assistant only to discover that there was about thirty large boxes of goods which had to be moved before we could reach the grill and the letters. The assistants were very kind.

In my own time I was enjoying progress with my interest in radio by reading the monthly magazine Practical Wireless. There was no other technical help available to me. I had built my first 0-V-0 valve radio. This was a simple receiver consisting of one valve used as a detector with some "re-action". To explain the 0-V-0 symbol, a 1-V-1 receiver for example, would be a detector valve with an additional valve before and after the detector to improve amplification. Re-action was a means of adjusting the circuit feedback almost to the point of oscillation where, just at this point, the sensitivity of the circuit is increased many times so that weak signals could be heard. Unusually, my 1224A communications receiver also had a re-action control, a facility not normally found in high grade receivers. I remember switching on my 0-V-0 receiver for the first time and hearing in the earphones Guy Mitchell singing "She Wears Red Feathers and a Hula Hula Skirt" coming through loud and clear on the Light Programme. The year was 1953.

All of the ac mains wiring of the day, at our house in 6 Queensway, consisted of twisted flex hanging down from a rose in the centre of the ceiling with a bayonet type bulb-holder fitted on the end. All of the electrical parts such as bulb-holder and ceiling rose, were made using an insulating material called

Bakelite, a material which could be moulded (thermo-set) and lightly machined. A modern light bulb would fit the early bulb-holder since the socket dimensions have hardly changed. The light bulb, smoothing iron and kitchen radio were all fed off the one bulb-holder by a three-way bayonet adapter. There was no earth or ground return so the system was highly dangerous. The twin flex was standard stuff, each half consisting of strands of wire covered in rubber with an overlay of reddish coloured cotton fabric weave. When connecting to a bulb holder, for example, the rubber and the cotton weave was stripped back to reveal the wires which were then threaded into the brass contacts and screwed down. The outer cotton weave would fray when it was trimmed so it was usually tightly bound using a black insulation tape.

Unfortunately this tape had a tendency to dry out and unfurl, dropping down on to the hot light bulb where it would first smoke profusely and then burst into flame. The rubber covering around the wires in the "flex" would also dry out and crumble often leading to short circuits.

Nevertheless, I had managed to secure a feed for myself from the house to the shed where I could have a light of my own, use an electric soldering iron and use my power supplies for my experiments. My interest in radio was growing and my 1224A communications receiver was traded in for an R1155E which had been adapted to work from the mains supply. In real life this set was used together with the T1154 transmitter in aircraft such as the Lancaster bomber for mission communications using Morse code.

To get my own amateur radio licence I would need to be proficient at sending and receiving code, and be technically competent in radio theory to the extent that I would know what I was doing if I put a transmitter on the air. Both Morse and theory would be tested by examination – no easy thing for me to contemplate, but at least I was making a start with the Morse.

This strange language isn't relevant today. Sea going radio operators don't need to know it and radio amateurs can obtain a licence without it. The maximum receiving speed ever known is 72 words per minute with a sending speed of 35 wpm using a normal Morse key observed in 1942.

My ability to read Morse coded signals was developing at a slow rate. It was reckoned that a person needed to hear a character sent in code 1000 times before it is easily recognised by the brain. In my case it was proving to be something like 5000 times. As I rode into school on my bicycle I would focus on the advertising hoardings by the side of the road and send selected words to myself in Morse such as da-dit-da-dit, dit-dit and so on, looking back over my shoulder as I sailed by endeavouring to complete a word before it went out of sight.

Unfortunately I did this once too often. I mounted the kerb, crashed into the pavement, buckled the bike, and badly injured my leg.

Peter Jones, G3ESY, GW5VX, GW3FVI, G2DFL and many other *radio amateurs* were always active on the allocated *ham bands* and they often joined the net at 11am on Sunday mornings on the 40-metre band. They could also be heard using Morse code a mastery of which, at least 12 words per minute, was mandatory before a transmitting licence could be issued. The usual procedure when transmitting Morse code was, and still is, to send your station call sign several times, including that of the other station, which gave me the chance to identify both.

My brother Bryan had become interested in printing and for a while I had to share the shed with his Adana printing press, trays of lead type pieces, inks, stocks of paper and cardboard of all kinds, until he found a room in Offa Street near St Peter's Square. My friend Cecil Adcocks also became interested and came to our house regularly to get involved and help Bryan. Cecil was to make printing his life and eventually set up his own company called Print Plus with premises in Widemarsh Street. Today, Print Plus is a successful, fully-computerised company producing all manner of printed material. I didn't know it at the time but printing and type-setting was to be a part of my life, too, in time to come.

In our house at 6 Queensway we spent a good deal of time in the evenings gathered around the fireplace in the kitchen reading and listening to the radio. On Fridays, after school, I would collect the comics from Turvy's the paper shop on the way home. The comics never changed and always consisted of the Beano, Dandy, Hotspur and Champion, the stories in the latter two really helping me to read. Later we included the Eagle which featured Dan Dare taking on the green Mekons. The Eagle was something different. It had a good crisp feel and look to it with exciting illustrations in shiny bold colours throughout, you wouldn't call it a comic like the other weeklies. These finished with, I would listen to the radio to the Dick Barton, special agent, omnibus with his pals Jock Anderson and Snowy White getting into, and getting out of, impossible situations.

The kitchen fire had a back boiler and to have constant hot water it would always need to be kept alight. However, when lighting the fire in the first place it was necessary to get a good up-draught of air through the grate, to make the coal, wood, tinder and paper catch fire. To really get it going I discovered that an opened-out newspaper spread across the mouth of the chimney had the desired effect but in seconds the flames would be reaching half way up the chimney and a quick reaction was required to remove it. On one occasion I wasn't quick enough and the newspaper caught fire. I dropped it and it fell onto the hearth and then the mat and in no time everything including the adjacent chairs were on fire. Bowls of water from the kitchen sink did the trick and the secondary fire was soon out. My parents went crazy and I didn't try to draw the fire that way again.

During the school summer holidays I would cycle with friends Gerald and Ken, to the CWS fruit farms to pick plums at Sutton St. Nicholas. We did this for at least a week to earn money, arriving at 8 o'clock in the morning and work until about 4.30pm. They were hot summer days just right for the wasps and bees also in attendance around the plums which were mainly Czars, large purple and juicy.

On our first day the foreman said "eat as many as you like lads, eat as many as you like" but we soon found that it was not possible to eat many without getting a stomach ache. He knew a thing or two about plums and the pickers. We each had a ladder which had to be manoeuvred amid the branches of the plum tree to reach the fruit. Payment, about a shilling a tray, was made at the end of the day when all of your trays were assessed but as you moved along the orchard you had to keep one eye over your shoulder, upon your tower of boxes below, because one or two had a habit of going missing – or, in my case, perhaps I couldn't add-up or remember properly.

Other summer days were spent by the river. Hereford has two, the Lugg and the Wye, which converge at a small hamlet called Mordiford just three miles southeast of the city. After joining at Mordiford, the river continues as the Wye. In those days the river water, especially the Lugg, was crystal clear in the shallows with dark green tufted riverbed weeds streaming in the current, a far cry from the brown slime that discolours the river flora today.

Different locations on the Lugg had local names such as the "the bulls horn" and "the hook" but the Lugg meanders and the course is much different today and the names long forgotten. A good day by the river would involve cutting down the rushes and making a raft on which we boys could sit and drift downstream, my dog Pip running along keeping pace on the bank. Fishing stories abound such as the man who caught a pike in the Lugg which, when landed, twisted around and bit the fisherman on his calf clinging on tightly. It was usual too, to help with the haymaking on the Lugg meadows to the south of the river. The help was given freely but the real lure was the farmer's cider which was available in great quantities.

Ever interested in radio I joined the 124 Squadron Air Training Corps with headquarters based in Eign Road. This dedicated building was a single-storey unit prefabricated from precast cement beams and cement blocks with wooded rooms to the rear. Inside there were offices, equipment store rooms and a small kitchen near an open area where the parades were held.

For me the allure was the chance to get Morse code practice in a properly equipped room. The equipment was an Airforce tone generator with ten Morse keys distributed along three tables in one of the wooden rooms at the rear of the building. The tutors were all amateur radio enthusiasts, my friend Peter Jones G3ESY, Peter Buchan G3INR and Roy Smith who eventually became G3MPB, all gave their time freely.

As well as Morse equipment there was also radio equipment such as T1154 transmitter and an Army No 12 transmitter and an HRO receiver. With the help of the radio amateurs the cadets were able to join the ATC net which involved other squadrons across the country. Procedure was highly orchestrated and you could only transmit when the control station passed the sequence over to you and then you would tap out your message knowing that the rest of the ATC Wing was listening.

The ATC organised summer camps and flying experience. For the latter the squadron went to RAF Shawbury, an airfield in Shropshire, for the day. We were given flights in an Anson aircraft. This aeroplane was designed before the war and was originally intended for coastal patrol. It had two engines with a maximum speed of well under 200mph. Our aircraft was fitted out for aircrew training and it had seating for about nine people plus pilot and co-pilot and the trip lasted an hour.

One evening when I was closing the windows at the ATC headquarters I inadvertently put the cigarette I was smoking onto my lips the wrong way around. I will never forget the most dreadful pain of it; for a lighted cigarette is the most concentrated source of heat for its size and the lips are the most sensitive part of the body. I had to pull the cigarette away from my lips dragging burned tissue as I did so. My lips healed somewhat over the course of two weeks but during this time I was in constant agony from the slightest lip movement.

My dad's fish and chip shop was a purpose-built prefabricated building at the top of the hill on College Green. It was about a quarter of a mile to walk to the shop from the house in 6 Queensway. Late in 1953 we moved to a prefabricated bungalow, number 34, directly opposite the shop. My brother Bryan had already left home and was living in Cardiff to be near his employers Olivetti, the typewriter company. The two grandfathers had also moved away to stay with other relatives.

This bungalow was a revelation since it had convection heating and a nice little kitchen with a refrigerator. I was particularly happy about the move because being at the top of the hill, 500 feet above sea level, I was able to get rather good radio reception using a long wire aerial strung out across the large garden. We bought our first radiogram, a Kolster Brandes, when we moved in. This would play 78 rpm records and receive broadcast stations in the Long , Medium and Short Wave bands. Our record collection included Doris Day singing the Deadwood Stage from the film Calamity Jane and Eddie Calvert, the man with the golden trumpet, playing Cherry Pink and Apple Blossom White. My own favourites were Louis Bellson featured in Skin Deep and Gene Krupa featured in Benny Goodman's Sing Sing Sing, terrific drumming.

One of my school mates, Tony Weldon, was also interested in radio. He lived in the south of Hereford, in Greyfriars. We both had communication receivers and by this time, had both constructed illicit radio transmitters. The transmitters were identical. Both used a single 6L6 valve and an F243 quartz crystal which resonated at a given frequency, in our case 6.090Mhz, and radiated some 5 watts of RF power. This power is enough to go half way around the world given the right frequency, and aerial, so we were ever hopeful that we didn't create interference and that the authorities wouldn't hear us.

Communication was by very slow Morse code sent to each other, usually on Saturday mornings, and again in the late afternoon. Although our signals were very strong in the morning they were very weak later on and much affected by fading. In this way, by experimenting, both of us learned first-hand about the effect called "skip". At this frequency radio waves are reflected back to earth by the ionosphere which shifts in height during the course of the day and night, consequently the point of best reception can move further away.

First communications receiver R1224A

Second communications receiver R1155E
(as used in the Lancaster bomber)

Third communications receiver R107 (Army)

With a glut of ex-government radio equipment around I traded in my receivers for different models. The 1224 for the 1155E which itself was replaced later by the R107 paid for from the proceeds of my evening paper round which I developed from scratch around Tupsley, a parish to the east of the city. The paper was called the Citizen and I earned five shillings on a good week when the weather was fine and people would stop me and buy one. I always carried extra for this purpose. This set was heavy and needed two people to lift it. Next, along came HRO receiver manufactured by the American company National. The Americans fought the war with the help of superb and innovative equipment and this set was no exception. My receiver was the standard model which had four plug-in coil units which covered the range 1.7MHz to 30MHz. The tuning dial was calibrated like a micrometer and was velvet smooth, a truly world-class piece of equipment and I was very lucky to have it.

Other receivers I acquired were the BC348 and the AR88D, also fine examples of American engineering and know-how. The former used by the American Air Force in heavy aircraft, covering 1.5MHz to 18MHz, and the latter produced by RCA covering 535KHz to 32MHz. The size and weight of the AR88D generally precluded operation from an aircraft for it weighed in at 100lb.

One of the business side-lines my dad had was a shop for the hop-pickers during the season at one of the local hop farms. He sold staples such as tinned food and groceries which were pre packed. He would also take orders for wet fish for delivery next day but only with cash pre-payment. During the season, the pickers would arrive from Wales in bus loads and stay at the farm. Dad had staff running his shop in Hereford which gave him the chance to be in attendance and sometimes I would go with him. The hop varieties had wonderful names such as Goldings and Fuggles. The pickers used to strip the vines by hand putting the hops into a large crib. Every so often the tractor, trailer and tally man would come by for the hops in the crib. These were measured out by the basket or bushell and put into the trailer and registered for payment at the end of the week.

One day at the farm I went walkabout and explored a tunnel underneath one of the hop curing kilns. As I went to the far end, a labourer turned up and set fire to a tray of yellow sulphur bars in the middle of the tunnel underneath a vent in the ceiling. When the sulphur burns it combines with the air to produce sulphur dioxide which is supposed to drift upwards and cure the hops above. In my predicament I couldn't help breathing the gas as I ran out. My chest seemed to contract and I could hardly breathe. Barely able to survive I lay stricken on the grass verge gasping for dear life. After twenty minutes or so my chest cleared itself and I started to regain composure. Able to breathe once more I cleared off in a state of shock.

It was early 1955. At school the O-level examinations were imminent and all of the eligible students were involved in mock examinations. After the mocks the headmaster Mr Roscoe called me to his study and explained that he thought that it was not worthwhile for me to sit the O-levels as he was quite sure I wouldn't pass any. I think, too, that he wanted to protect his beloved school from criticism from the examiners.

However, I think Mr Roscoe genuinely wanted to help me. He asked me what my interests were and what I thought I might now do under the circumstances. I told him that I was keen on radio and that I belonged to Hereford 124 Squadron ATC. Beyond this I didn't have any idea. He suggested that I join the Royal Air Force as an apprentice and try to get acceptance to No1 Radio School based at Locking near Weston Super Mare. He said to think about it for a few days and to then let him know. After discussing it with mum and dad I agreed that this would be the best for me. From this point on Mr Roscoe liaised with the Air Force authorities who sent through to the school their own examination papers for me to sit. He also gave me some limited advice and personally attended while I did the examination.

I passed the exam and subsequently a travel warrant arrived for me to attend RAF Halton for a thorough medical. It was thorough and I had to stay overnight. One of the tests was to assess hearing ability. In a long room, one nurse stood at one end while I and another nurse were standing at the other end. My nurse cupped each of my ears in turn while the other spoke words for me to try and hear. The test was deemed successful but the results became a matter for conjecture in years to come. I gained entrance to the Air Force and I wasn't yet 17 years old. What would I make of this turn of fortune I wondered?

FROM THE BOTTOM OF THE CLASS

Chapter 3

The Royal Air Force

Well, here I am at *Camp Grenada*, the Apprentice wing of No1 Radio School, Royal Air Force Locking, located eight miles east of Weston-super-Mare, Somerset. It is the afternoon of Tuesday 4th September 1955, I am not yet 17 and I am wondering what the hell I have let myself in for. My dad had said goodbye to me at Hereford railway station and I made my way to Weston-super-Mare changing trains at Bristol Temple Meads, the trip paid for by a military travel warrant. It was made out for a one-way trip.

At Weston railway station there were several grey Royal Air Force lorries and buses lined up to collect me and my new friends-to-be upon our arrival and whisk us off to the camp. An assortment of military police and drill sergeants with lists and clip-boards were on hand to greet us, take our details, and guide us to the vehicles – they were very nice.

The afternoon was warm and sunny and when my bus arrived at the camp everyone seemed to be playing sports. Apparently, Tuesday afternoon was reserved for sports every week. Our flight commander-to-be, Flt Lt Rippon, dressed in a maroon track suit, introduced himself and greeted us as we stepped down from the bus. I was shown to a bed in hut number 354, a wooden habitat which was to be my home for the next three years. It didn't bear thinking about, so I tried not to.

All of this was undeserved and not very well thought out. I just seemed to be doing what was expected of me, doing the grown-up thing you might say, so I set out to let it wash over me and attempted to stay honest.

I was one of 129 young men making up the latest intake known as the 81st Entry of RAF Apprentices of whom only 54 eventually passed out three years later. There were three squadrons A, B, and C, each with three entries. My entry went into C squadron signified by a silver hat band on our dress head gear. The A squadron wore a blue hat band and B squadron wore a green hat band. In total there were nine entries under training, we were obviously the junior guys and the new senior Entry was the 73rd in A squadron.

We were the replacement for C squadron 72nd entry who had just passed out at the end of the previous summer term, occupying the huts recently vacated by them.

My new friends turned out to have almost all been previous members of the Air Training Corps and had a desire to be in the RAF. All appeared to be well educated and most had O-level qualifications. We all looked fit and there were no obese young men among the intake.

In this military institution everything and everybody had a name and a number. Everything taught by a procedure which could not be altered – everything from bedtimes to the firing of machine guns. It was all part of a highly-specified process.

681398 Bush M.A.

The Apprentices were quite separate from the enlisted men, conscripts, also known to us as "bogmen", and had their own hierarchy of NCOs drawn from the most able of the senior apprentices.

There were Sergeant Apprentices with three stripes on their sleeve, Corporal Apprentices who had two stripes and Leading Apprentices with one stripe, all of them were powerful and demanded obedience and respect from us sprogs.

The huts were also known as billets and each housed 24 men plus a Leading Apprentice from a senior entry. In our billet the LA was called Tin Mung from Burma. We quickly renamed him Tin Mug. There were a few dozen foreign students scattered among the multitude in the wing no doubt destined for special positions in the military in their own countries.

Starting at the top, the professional commissioned officers looking after us included a Wing-Commander, Three Squadron-Leaders, and nine Flight-Lieutenants. The Wing Commander reported to the Station Commander who was a Group Captain. The professional NCOs were answerable to the WO-Man as he was known.

This was the wing warrant officer who we quickly learned was also called the "grass monkey" being a little man with a large dress hat two sizes too big and a voice to match. He was always seen with his grey bike either pushing it or riding it – the bike too, being far too big for him.

Each squadron had a drill sergeant and a drill corporal who were answerable to the wing flight sergeant who liaised with the "grass monkey". Our drill sergeant was sergeant String, a small portly man with a ruddy face who could change his temperament in a moment. He would get his instructions from Squadron Office. He was the only professional man in constant contact with us and with direct responsibility for our turn-out and welfare.

September 5th and 6th were days occupied with a gentle induction into camp life. We were shown the NAAFI which was across the road from our billets. Here you could buy tea, coffee, cakes, sandwiches and limited cooked food; also soft drinks and cigarettes – but not alcohol. The tables and chairs were basic with seating arranged four to a table. You could enjoy a smoke, a pleasure which was not allowed outside or in our billet accommodation and a good sing-song around the piano played by my good friend John "boots" Dallimore who later became a Group Captain in the Royal Australian Air Force. John received his RAF commission in 1963 and retired in 1976. Within two weeks he had moved to Australia and joined the RAAF which was all prearranged while he was seconded to the MOD. My entry also produced one Wing Commander three Squadron Leaders, of which several were Welshmen and formidable rugby players, and a host of other officers.

There were films about RAF life and activities and interesting films about aircraft shown to us at the Astra – the forces organisation of cinemas. We spent a long time getting fitted out with kit comprising everything from pyjamas to gabardine raincoat, and a peculiar thing called a "housewife". This was a folded pouch which contained all of the parts to darn socks and to sew things, with spare buttons and so on.

Life for these few days was relaxed and carefree. Food at the mess hall was good with plenty available. Generally it was a main course and a sweet followed by a selection of jams to have with bread and butter. Tea was always on tap from several urns placed at the front of the mess. At supper-time this was replaced by hot chocolate with more bread, butter and jam if you wanted it. We were issued with a large mug, knife, fork and spoon, almost as soon as we arrived at the camp and at the end of a meal would be responsible for washing our eating irons thoroughly in a bath of hot scalding water.

During the fateful morning of Friday September the 7th we were assembled in the NAAFI for a talk and blessing from the camp padre, an officer who had special duties to look after our spiritual welfare. Then we were each given forms, a military agreement, with our names typed across the top and told to sign on the dotted line below. I dutifully signed mine and committed the next 12 years of my life to the RAF. I knew in my heart that this was an act of closure on my life as I had known it, and that from now on, things would never be the same again. I was an enlisted man.

Immediately after the signing we were sent back to our billets, in my case hut 354 where Tin Mug was waiting to receive me and my new friends. Tin Mug ranted and raved at us rather like the Vietcong goading Robert De Niro in the film The Deer Hunter. We were scheduled for haircuts almost straight away. In the hut we had to wear floor-pads under our shoes for the next year to protect the floor which initially was left in a poor state by the recently departed 73rd entry. These guys had also left fish to rot under the wooden lockers when they departed as a legacy for us upon our arrival.

The immediate objective was to train each recruit to become an obedient servant to the military cause. This was achieved by stripping away all vestiges of the former "self" and self-respect, rebuilding the person with disciplined, military values leaving the personality barely intact.

With the passage of time, I tried to cope with these changes as best as I could. Knowing that I was being turned into someone different I trusted that I would become a worthwhile person somewhere along the journey. I had my doubts.

Incessant obsession with shiny polished floors, dust and highly polished brass effects such as cap badges, became the prime concern for the year to come. Pressed uniform, carefully blancoed belts, polished boots with mirror finished toe-caps, and beds (blankets and sheets) perfectly formatted, were all part of the regime known as "bull shit", or simply "bull".

The condition of the floor had to be perfect and in the evenings we were put to work with large tins of polish, working it into the linoleum by swinging "bumpers" to and fro. These implements consisted of a heavy metal shoe, lined with bristles, which swivelled on the end of a heavy broom-like handle. With the beds moved out of the way, the polish application was followed by the first attempt to get a shine by using folded pieces of derelict blanket material under the bumper head. The second stage involved small teams of guys on their hands and knees buffing up the shine with elbow grease. There was great enthusiasm, believe it or not, I guess we were all in it together and we made the best of it.

As we worked, dressed in our overalls, we sang the songs of the day such as Cool Water by Frankie Laine and The Yellow Rose of Texas. And, perhaps more apt, Sixteen Tons by Tennessee Ford.

On a week-day we would be woken at 6.30am to get dressed, make the bed and assemble the folded blankets and sheets to form a perfect blanket-pack of the correct dimensions at precisely the correct place at the head end of the bed.

Clutching our mug and irons we would march to the mess hall and back in groups for breakfast for we were not yet allowed to walk to the mess. Afterwards it was necessary to assemble outside the squadron huts at 8.45am to march down en-masse to the technical wing. If the weather was cold we would wear our greatcoats and gloves, if it was raining, then we draped a square of waterproof material about our person issued to us for this purpose.

At the outset, our training began with general studies, English, maths, electrical theory, radio principles and workshop instruction – electronics hadn't then been invented. The curriculum was based upon the ONC, Ordinary National Certificate, which for me was like jumping out of the frying pan into the fire. I couldn't memorise anything but I clearly had this second chance to try. Some instructors were officers and others were civilian but they all taught with dedication and they were tolerant. The workshop classes were brilliant and we were taught to recognise materials and tools, and how to use everything from a rasp file to a lathe. There was technical drawing instruction with projects which we would develop from drawing to finished product.

In the workshop, towards the end of the first year, we started to work on a major radio project. This was the manufacture of all of the parts, except the valves, for a medium and long-wave wireless set, wiring up the circuit and subsequently testing and aligning it. We were instructed in everything from marking out, punching and folding the sheet-metal chassis through to turning composite coil-formers and winding the coils onto them.

All of this was top-drawer training and I discovered that workshop practice suited me very well because it was soon obvious to me that I could learn by doing which was for me, a distinct progress.

September 14 was my first pay day. I was paid 7/6d per week but 2/6d was compulsory savings. In the second year we were paid 17/6d and in the third year 21/6d. The savings were paid out together with our compounded wages before we departed for annual holidays – it was a tidy sum to go home with in those days. Lining up in front of the paying officer

Top view, bottom view. Photos of apprentice's superhet radio showing variable capacitors, coils and transformers, all hand made.

Photos courtesy of Peter Moore and Tony Mooney.

and pay clerk, on my turn, I would jump forward, come to attention, salute and quote my "1250" pass number and my personal number, in my case, 150358 and 681398 respectively. The pay was handed over and during the process you were scanned by the drill sergeant for neatness and quality of haircut.

There were three 48-hour passes supported with train travel warrants per year, one for each term. It was possible to get additional 48-hour passes if you had a good excuse, but they were not supported by a travel warrant. Excuses were generally to do with dying relatives, funerals and other compassionate matters. I could get home to Hereford quite easily but some of my friends lived in Northern Ireland and the Isle of Man and so they wouldn't go home until the main holidays arrived.

Return travel warrants were also issued at the end of each term for the holidays and we were taken to Weston railway station in an organised bussing system. At Temple Meads I headed for the bar for a few drinks and to pass the time while waiting for my connection. It was quite usual to see many service personnel in uniform in those days. I was in uniform, too, and I had to beware of the Military Police always on patrol in the station who might pull me up for underage drinking.

Time went by slowly in the squadron. There were always inspections at night and on Saturday mornings for three weekends out of four. Then there were all manner of parades and drill training sessions – learning to march and react to commands in unison.

The major event was the AOCs parade (Air Officer Commanding) usually taken by a visiting Air Commodore. I hated parades, it was a time thing again, I could never come to terms with the prospect of standing rooted to the spot for hours on end, sometimes at-ease but mostly stiffly at attention. I used to sweat and palpitate each time with anxiety and fear that I might fall over in a fainting fit, working myself up into a kind of panic a day or so before the parade.

This went on for years and though I never did faint, it must have affected my nervous system somewhat. I would try and dodge parade by reporting sick although this wasn't always possible.

One of the common reported complaints I used was athlete's foot. I would arrive at sick bay and join the others sitting around with their feet immersed in baths of a purple solution of potassium permanganate and warm water. This was skiving I soon learned but I wasn't happy about it. We always had the Station Medical Officer on our side, she was a lady with the rank of Squadron Leader who drove an open-top green sports-model Bugatti which you could hear all over the camp when she was out and about.

During my first year I started doing haircuts for 3d a time. I became quite adept at it and I was kept busy during the evenings when it was not practical to go to the camp barber. On the downside I had a direct line to the drill sergeant who blamed me every time a colleague looked in need of a short back and sides. I used two pairs of mechanical clippers plus normal scissors but my friend Alan Ball in the billet next door had electric clippers and he was my competition. In the most dreadful of circumstances he was killed using the tool. His clippers were connected to the light socket in the ceiling which was not properly earthed as wall sockets are today. It was early winter and someone shouted that the central heating had been turned on, Alan was holding the clippers when he bent down to feel the pipes on the billet wall and was electrocuted. Unlike today no one knew about immediate resuscitation aid and although the hospital was a short distance away there was no telephone, so when assistance finally did arrive it was too late, he was dead. We were all very upset.

The first year was hard. I was always polishing to get the required gleam on brass parts and boots, and pressing to get the sharpest of creases in the arms and legs of my uniform. The toe caps of my boots were polished in small circular movements using a finger and a small piece of cloth for hours on end. This treatment of the leather eventually led to a mirror-like shine and was a record of the persistence and character of the individual. Boots were sacrosanct and the shine greatly protected from damage – woe betide other students with careless feet. Brass effects were belt buckles and cap badges which were polished with Duraglit so often that the metal became smooth and soft yellow.

For the vaguest of reasons the junior entries were set upon by the more senior entries generally for small verbal assaults on the hierarchy. The usual method was for them to work their way through the billets tipping every bed and its sleeping occupant onto the floor in the middle of the night. I survived numerous raids which not only produced stunned bewilderment but generally wrecked the previous evening's efforts of bull shit thus producing a double whammy.

After the first six months in year one we were allowed to have the radio on at 11pm on a Sunday night, even though lights-out was at 10pm, in order to listen to the top 20 programme on Radio Luxemburg, on 208 metres found at the low end of the medium wave. Presenters of the day included David Jacobs and Pete Murray. Then, Skiffle became very popular and we formed our own group consisting of John Dallimore on the guitar, me on the wash-board and John Rossindale on the improvised bass which consisted of an upside down tea chest, a broom handle, and string. It was always great fun playing Lonnie Donnegan tunes such as The Rock Island Line and many others.

The Apprentices' wing had a hobbies centre which was housed in the IDH block, Infectious Diseases Hospital, which was a multi-roomed, well-built single-storey building which had never been used for the purpose for which it was intended. Within its walls there was the model aero club, printing club, woodwork club and amateur radio club G3IDZ. Other rooms were used for swotting before exams and also for budding musicians like us.

Cliques of like-minded students would assemble to brain-storm their way through texts and class notes for hours on end but as always there were the successful ones who never needed to revise. These were the smart guys who were promoted to NCOs. Although I admired their qualities I could never understand what they gained from promotion since there were no special privileges and they all ended up with extra responsibilities and doing twice as much work as anyone else.

G3IDZ was a well-equipped amateur radio station and I spent a lot of time there. The transmitter was constructed by the senior apprentices and had a DC power of 50 watts when using Morse code and 20 watts when using voice. The aerials were multi-band types hoisted some 40 feet in the air. For receiving there was an American AR88. I was able to use the G3IDZ call, supposedly under supervision, to get first-hand Morse practice and general radio experience.

I still treasured the thought that someday I would get my own amateur radio licence and this came together in my second year. I was able to sit my Morse examination at G8FC, the Royal Air Force amateur radio headquarters on the camp site, where an approved Sergeant wireless operator set the 12 wpm tests. I passed first time.

The GPO regulatory body also granted technical licences to 2nd year RAF Locking Apprentices without the need for further examination if the candidate had completed his second year radio principles exam. My licence was duly applied for and in late September 1957 I received a note that there was a registered letter waiting for me at the Wing post office. Skipping lunch I hurried over there and to my lasting glee and joy my licence had arrived. I had been given the call sign G3LZM. Using my own phonetics this would become G-3-London-Zanzibar-Mexico for evermore.

My licence registered address was my home in Hereford but by putting the suffix "/A" after my call sign (G3LZM/A) I could legally use the G3IDZ equipment. My very first contact was with VE3BHS, Bob in Port Arthur, Canada, made on October 1 and subsequently my friend in Hereford, Peter Jones

Mike's radio station G3LZM located in Hereford in 1975.

G3ESY, on October 6. Full of enthusiasm I started to build a transmitter and modulator (for voice) at the club to take home with me when the Christmas holidays arrived. Italian products were quite popular at that time especially scooters. I ordered through the post a Geloso transmitter VFO unit (variable frequency oscillator) to form the heart of my new rig which was to use an 807 power amplifier valve feeding an adjustable Pi section antennae loading circuit.

Not content with my home made transmitter I opted to buy something altogether bigger for Christmas and ordered a Panda Explorer costing £90. This transmitter had a DC power of 120 watts generated by a pair of 6146 valves. In retrospect these valves should have been designed into the unit with a fan for forced-air cooling to prevent overheating.

When I arrived home for Christmas 1957 my dad drove me to Manchester to the Panda Radio Company to collect the Explorer. With this set and my location at home on top of the College Estate hill in Hereford, I guessed I would be able to put out a world-class signal and this proved to be the case. I received top reports from all areas as far afield as Japan.

Another important milestone was 1957 which was IGY, the International Geophysical Year. At the time I obtained my radio licence the Russian satellite Sputnik 1 was sent into space with low earth orbit. This was the start of the space race and it sent jitters throughout the western world. It is normal for radio amateurs to send a card (QSL) to confirm a contact. The card would carry the contact details and the call sign of the other party. Cards would be sent in batches to the Radio Society of Great Britain (RSGB) for onward posting free of charge. The cards were about post-card size and often had lovely designs and pictures featured with the station call sign. For my new QSL I chose a picture of Sputnik and the initials IGY with my G3LZM call also printed on it. Contact details would be filled in on the other side.

By the end of the second year various changes had taken place which reflected our growing seniority. We didn't have to march in groups down to the mess hall any longer and we could wear shoes more often. The perpetual cleaning and polishing had eased off considerably. For ceremonial parades we were each given a Lee Enfield .303 rifle and long chrome plated bayonet. While the bayonet and the highly polished scabbard was kept in the locker, the rifles with firing pins removed, were chained up at the end of the billet when not in use.

We called the rifles "Gats" which I suppose was short for Gatling gun. There were scares from time to time from the IRA. When these occurred the camp siren would sound and a special guard was mounted over the rifles in the senior billets.

The bolt-action .303 had been the basic British infantry weapon for 50 years. Its durability and accuracy were legendary but it was becoming rapidly out of date by the time we were issued with it. However it is still in use in some parts of the world today.

Emerging music of the day was essentially "rock-n, roll" led in 1956 by Bill Haley with Rock Around the Clock. In 1957 there was a kind of liberated feeling in the air which we apprentices could not really take part in. The Teddy Boy culture had taken off and gangs from Bristol would raid Weston-super-Mare on the weekends causing mayhem, often assaulting Apprentices who would be in town dressed in uniform. For our own protection we were given classes in self-defence by the camp physical training instructors. They trained us in several ways to defend ourselves but particularly by using the forearm to smack the offender hard across the throat which, we were warned, could be near-lethal.

During the summer holidays in our second year a group of six of us consisting of me, Al Chiddicks, Ken Pugh, Roy Auger, Frank Clines and his friend Bob Mattox, hired a boat for a week's holiday on the Norfolk Broads. My aunty Glad had run up a special black flag with 81 in large white numbers sewn onto each side for us to fly. We all met at Coltishall, near to the famous RAF station, to pick up the boat which was a six-berth cruiser. We were briefed about the boat and the right-of-way laws of the Broads. Nearer Great Yarmouth the waters were tidal and we were shown how to moor the craft to take account of the rise and fall. At Great Yarmouth we met three girls on the beach and invited them back to the boat for a meal. I insisted that we put glasses of water on the table only to see for the first time that there were pieces floating around in the glasses. It turned out that we had been using river water for drinking and ablutions because the wrong water tap had been turned on.

The river water carried raw sewage especially around Yarmouth for it was common in those days to discharge effluent directly out of the craft whereas today it is illegal to discharge into the water on lakes and canals, a procedure replaced by efficient chemical toilets.

There were several occasions during the holiday where we engaged with girls, some locals and some also on holiday. No liaisons were formed but it was good fun just flirting, drinking and smoking. We all had a great time.

During 1957 the squadron was handed over to the loving care of the RAF Regiment for two weeks of battlefield training. The Regiment consisted of professional armed soldiers formed to defend airfields and their installations. We were transported from Locking to a very basic camp near miles of sand dunes somewhere near RAF Chivenor on the Taw estuary in North Devon and into the hands of professional NCOs led by a noisy Flight Sergeant we called "Nagasaki". He was so called because he was supposed to have witnessed the atom bomb falling on the town in Japan as a captive in a far-off prison. He had a head shaped like a coconut with a crew-cut and a mean, thin grin.

Always shouting at us, he and his mob gave us a hard time. We were formed into platoons for exercises and manoeuvres and as he scanned my platoon he said looking at me with a wry grin that it was normal for the smallest man to carry the heavy machine gun. The others thought that made good sense and laughed as I struggled with my kit, the 10kg Bren gun and magazines of blank cartridges.

The Bren was another WWII weapon rapidly becoming out of date. It had, however, an illustrious history and was sometimes criticised for being too accurate as a burst was concentrated rather than spread over a wide area.

Our basic accommodation was in small WW1 Nissen huts over which we had to mount guard day and night in "watches" and take on other duties. We hardly had any sleep and it was in this perpetual state of tiredness that we manoeuvred. A typical exercise was called a "lamp snatch" which took place in the middle of the night. This consisted of trainees being divided into two groups. Each group had a lamp on a tall sand hill which they had to protect while at the same time sending out a patrol to capture the opposition's lamp. During the exercise the NCOs threw thunder flashes all over the place, scaring us to hell. Then they would run among us kicking and roughing us up.

Tired as we were, we were later taken out to sea in DUKWs for simulated beach landings. These were flat-bottomed boats as used in the D-day landings. The craft tossed and swayed uncontrollably in the ocean swell and many of us were sick.

In the middle of the second week the camp was smitten with the influenza pandemic, the Asian flu of 1957/58 which killed two million people world-wide. Among the casualties was Nagasaki. Word got around and we all lined up and jeered as he was stretchered away by the orderlies into a waiting ambulance. My glee was short-lived however, when next day I found myself among others being transported back to camp in an RAF ambulance and straight into hospital with a high fever and breathing problems. This flu was very infectious.

Back at RAF Locking, the Entry had been split into distinct classes according to our abilities for training on actual equipment. The cleverest went into the Radar Class, subsequently some of these guys went to Fylingdales, the secret Anglo-American early warning radar installation in North Yorkshire. The next group went into Air Radio which incorporated Air Radar. The last group were the less bright students and they went into Ground Radio which is where I ended up. I was trained on Creed Tele-printers, "very high frequency" and "high frequency" receivers and transmitters. The largest HF transmitter was 40kW. It was built into a structure rather like a room. It was so dangerous that if you had to go inside when it was shut down, you had to carry an earthing rod, rather like a shepherds crook with a cable to earth, to place on the large power supply capacitor terminals in order to make sure that they were properly discharged and safe. In operation the transmitter used a high tension of thousands of volts. Any residual voltage left on the capacitors after shut-down would be lethal if accidentally touched.

These transmitters and the lesser SWB transmitters, were mainly used for communication between England and the Commonwealth, and global command headquarters.

As part of the course training it was necessary for every senior Entry to write a thesis. It had to be at least 5000 words but could be on any topic. A corporal Apprentice in the 78th entry in our squadron chose Hypnosis as his theme. This caused great interest to many of us, me included, and I made a point of reading the booklets that were flying around. Apparently one method of taking over another person's mind was to get the subject to lie fully relaxed in a quiet situation and get him to concentrate on the diamond in the centre of an ace of diamonds from a pack of cards. He would hold the card in front of his eyes while the hypnotist talked him into falling asleep, if this is done with patience, he would be possessed. I tried being the hypnotist and there was no shortage of trusting friends ready to give it a go. Given that we were all tired at the end of the day anyway, it didn't take long for me to get success. I guess my dreary voice had as much to do with sending people off to sleep as the ace of diamond. I was able to make the subject stiffen his muscles so that he could span two chairs spaced apart using only the back of his head and ankles, a feat not possible to do normally. Some of my colleagues wanted to give up smoking and I was able to help with this by implanting the notion that cigarettes tasted and smelled disgusting. This worked well but the effect wore off after about two days.

In retrospect, in my innocence, I think I got away with experiments that could have had dangerous consequences.

My 81st entry was due to take final examinations in June 1958. We were the senior Entry on the Apprentices wing sporting an air of accomplishment and achievement. We no longer concerned ourselves with bull-shit and were allowed to go off camp in civilian clothes. These civvies were regulated and had to consist of grey trousers and black blazer with the Apprentices woven badge sewn onto the breast pocket. After the exams we just relaxed and did exactly as we wished as we waited for the results. It was a very warm summer and when we weren't playing volley ball we sun-bathed on top of the billets using olive oil as a sun-tan lotion which caused our skin to turn copper brown. The song of the moment was "I Was A Big Man" by the Four Preps, the song went on, "I was a big man yesterday but boy you ought to see me now!" If I passed the exams I would become a JT, a junior technician, with guaranteed promotion to Corporal Technician within three months.

I had made it this far with my feeble memory, but would I get through? Well, yes I did. I was greatly elated to be one of the few that made it, many of the original intake didn't. The 81st entry, or what was left of it, passed out on the 29th July 1958 in a massive review parade with bands, involving all of the Apprentice squadrons and parents with families who were also given a tour of the station.

My mother and father came to the parade and to the special dinner and dance arranged for the occasion at the Grand Hotel in Weston. The day after, I returned home to Hereford with them for a holiday, leaving behind a life I had known for three long years.

In September I took up my first posting. Using a travel warrant I made my way to RAF Henlow in Bedfordshire where I was to work in the Wireless Engineering Squadron (WES) repairing radio equipment. There were sand-coloured communications vehicles in for repair after being shot at during the Suez crisis which had started in October 1956.

The Suez crisis was the first indication after WWII that the Anglo-American special relationship was not all it was cracked up to be. Britain, France and Israel had invaded Egypt to protect their interests in the Suez canal but the affair was short lived when Eisenhower withdrew American support. Protest meetings against Prime Minister Eden were held in Britain. Nasser blocked the canal and petrol was rationed for a time in the UK.

My particular task was to repair American UHF transceivers which I had never seen before. I have raved about American equipment because it is so good and well-engineered for the time, and these units, with their intricate tuning mechanisms, were no exception. They all suffered from the same problem that in the transmitter section, a Perspex isolating block in the power amplifier compartment, would be breached by RF energy and had to be replaced. This was not an easy process because it involved dismantling the unit to get at the part.

Within a few months I was promoted and moved again to join an installation team in the Radio Installation Squadron (RIS) where I was to work alongside my good friend from RAF Locking, ex-Apprentice John Herring. At the time, the RAF was fitting ILS (Instrument Landing Systems) to suitable airfields and our job was to help the manufacturers (Marconi) with site assessments using a mobile American system and to assist with installation of the British ILS. One of the assessments was made at RAF West Malling and two installations I was involved with were RAF Leeming and RAF Leuchars in Fyfe, Scotland. I didn't feel particularly useful and I just supported John when needed which was just as well because most of it was above my head. In fact I was suffering from a large dose of "Imposter Syndrome" most of the time.

RAF Leuchars was most interesting. The airfield activity consisted of Lightning fighters and Javelin fighter-bombers taking off and landing all day long which, considering we were working alongside the runway, was a noisy nuisance and not entirely safe. So that we could be seen we wore white duffle coats. The airfield is on the coast surrounded by a pine forest which had ground-to-air missile installations dotted around in it. One day, after a gale at sea had blown itself out, we all went down to the beach to look at hundreds of jelly fish that had been washed up. There were all shades and colours from translucent to blue and many sizes, some three feet in diameter.

ILS allows an aircraft to distinguish between radio beams aimed into the sky at a fixed angle allowing it to make an approach in poor visibility. As part of the "tuning-up" procedure we relied on a specially equipped Varsity aircraft to make trials with dummy landings. It was on one of these occasions that my next big moment occurred. With the aircraft in the air, an adjustment was made with the "glide path" aerial wound down. After the adjustment, I was told by the party chief, a Warrant Officer, to crank the aerial back into position which I duly did but in doing so, I inadvertently severed one of the loose coaxial cables in the process. The trials were halted and the plane had to land. Apparently, someone called out "watch that cable" but I didn't hear the warning. This led to an inquisition of course and it transpired that I was going deaf. This was serious and I reported to Medical Officer back at RAF Henlow, our headquarters. I was sent to a services hearing centre in Warren Street in London for audiometry tests which proved that I was completely deaf in my right ear. There has never been an explanation for this and I was afraid that I might lose hearing in my left ear as well. The net result was that the authorities gave me two options. One, I could stay in the RAF but for only eight more years, and two, I could leave.

I chose the latter because clearly I wasn't going to be able to pursue a career and I was disenchanted with the formal Service life anyway. National Service was still in force and most of my charge were reluctant conscripts, many of them very well educated, or in higher education when called up, and I disliked telling them what to do. It was false.

From 1950 every man over the age of eighteen was expected to serve in the armed services for two years and remain on the reserve list for four years.

So by the time I was 21 years old on December 16th 1959 I had left the services and had arrived back where I started from – at home in Hereford. Now I had to find a proper job hopefully in industry working with up-to-date technology because at that time RAF equipment was at least five years out of date by the time it entered service.

Had I learned anything during my time in the services? I guess I had gained a sense of discipline and a strong sense of what is right and wrong but I also had a certificate of achievement, a technical document which listed everything I had been trained in, from Lister diesel-electric generating sets, to killing machines with all the Services radio equipment in between.

The 60's beckoned, time for me to shed the institution mantle and see what civilian life had in store for me in London.

Chapter 4

Living and Working in London

January 1960. I had no job so I immediately set about finding one for my parents were not the sort to countenance this situation for too long. I consulted the Daily Telegraph jobs section at the rear of the paper and noted that there were plenty of vacancies for overseas posts.

International Air Radio was always eager to place British engineers into posts in the Middle East and elsewhere, particularly in radio engineering and communications. In due course, these opportunities were taken by Fillipinos who were very competent and cost less.

I decided to deal with the top men in the game so I wrote to King Idris of Libya direct asking if his Ministry of Posts and Telecommunications had any vacancies. To my utter surprise I received an airmail packet from Libya with two large stamps in the right-hand corner. The stamps were franked and pictured desert views with date palm trees.

The letter instructed me to go to the Libyan Embassy in London and collect a work permit and travel warrant and make my way to Tripoli. The salary would be discussed at the Embassy but it would be tax-free and include subsistence money and generous paid holidays back in the UK. As it turned out, I didn't take up this offer but did get to Tripoli in later years by which time the king was overthrown and Colonel Gaddafi had taken over.

The only other letter I wrote was to J F Crosfield of Elthorne Road, Archway in north London. I had an admiration for the emerging technologies known as automation and I thought I would like to get involved if I could. Crosfields, so the advertisement ran, was a strong company in printing press automation and other related processes in the industry. These printing processes were to do with daily newspapers and glossy magazines, printing colour on giant rotogravure high-speed presses in Fleet Street.

In due course I was invited to an interview which was followed by an offer of a position as an installation engineer. I was to go on a three-week course to Norwood Technical College to study pulse techniques and then I was to attend the production test department to learn about the products before joining the installation team. My salary was to be £12 per week while at Norwood and then £700 a year. While abroad I would get a generous allowance of £3 per day to pay for the hotel and food and £2.10 per day when visiting customers in the UK. It was possible to live well in a hotel and still have money left over to boost my savings.

I was not able to start until the beginning of April so I found temporary employment with Heins and Co, a radio, television and music shop located in Broad Street. I worked in the radio servicing department with my good friend Ken Clegg whom I had known from four years ago when he joined me and my school pals drinking in the City Arms. Ken was an ex-army radio technician who had served in North Africa attached to a tank regiment. If I remember correctly he was instrumental in finding me this temporary job and later I was able to repay this kindness by offering him one in my own company, ETL Systems, after his business Kings Radio had to close down.

Ken was known as "uncle Ken" by my employees who valued his kindness and willingness to sort out production problems for them. We were all shocked and saddened when he died suddenly in November 2003 aged 64.

April arrived and I set off for London. Dennis Bent, the Technical Director of Crosfields had suggested that the company should pay my hotel expenses for a few weeks until I found accommodation so I stayed at the Pine Lodge in Highgate. Peggy Toft the company telephonist, a plump lady with rimmed glasses and a harelip, thought I might like to stay with her and her husband in their flat where they had a spare room. The accommodation was just across the road from the factory so I took up the offer. Her husband Sid was a carpenter and he was building an Andy Capp bar in the corner of the lounge. Andy Capp was the cartoon character created by Reg Smythe for the Daily Mirror and Sunday Mirror and had been running in these newspapers since 1957.

A northern working class layabout, drinker and pigeon fancier, Andy Capp was every-one's favourite and something of a cult character.

Sid was building his cocktail bar according to the published plans in the Mirror and when he had finished we had great pleasure stocking the shelves with beer, just as Andy would do, and christening it. Sid also made me a wooden box in which I could keep my growing collection of oil paint tubes, brushes and palette for I had taken up painting and completely lost interest in amateur radio for the time being. I was to find this friendliness everywhere in London and I warmed to it instantly.

After my course at Norwood I joined the test laboratory at the factory none the wiser. The work involved testing Autotron equipment and putting right any defects that may have occurred during production. The process suited me. I enjoyed working through a list of functions, or manipulations, according to a step-by-step written test procedure and checks. The way the test specification was written meant that I could deal with each stage at my own pace and by the end of the schedule the equipment would be ready for the next operation – the soak test.

The soak test involved keeping the equipment turned on for 48 hours before checking again for performance. When all of the tests were completed the equipment was sent to the dispatch department and subsequently to the customer. The circuits all used valves and each Autotron shelf unit had 20, consequently the amount of heat generated when large numbers of shelves were stacked together was considerable and forced-air cooling was employed.

The Autotron system was being sold world-wide. When installed on a four-colour printing press the method used scanning heads to look for colour register marks specially printed in the fold area of every page on the paper web. The colours were black and the three primary colours cyan (bright blue), magenta (a vivid red-purple) and yellow.

These were printed one at a time as the web travelled through the length of the press. If a colour was out of alignment the electronics would activate moving "register rollers" positioned high up between each printing bay to take up, or pay out, the moving paper by small amounts until the colours were back in register. The fast moving paper web would be subjected to different stresses including shrinkage due to the ink-drying process. The Crosfield system of electronics made sure that a perfect picture was printed whatever the conditions.

Among the other equipment which I had to test was the Trakatron. We are all familiar pulling a red or black thread on items like cigarette cartons to remove the cellophane wrapping. Well this small system controlled the alignment of the parent cellophane reel, pre-printed with red or black parallel lines, feeding a multiplicity of slitting knives to produce accurately cut thin sub-reels of "pull thread" destined for the packaging machines.

This was automation and I enjoyed being involved. I felt for the first time that I was making a positive contribution and getting paid well, so much so that I was able to buy my first tailored shirt, boxed and wrapped in cellophane, for £2.10 And, if I so chose, I could afford to go home to Hereford by train for the weekend for £4 return.

Getting home involved leaving work half an hour early on a Friday evening and getting a bus to

Mike working on a picture of Battersea Power Station
at Mrs Carter's lodgings.

Finsbury Park underground to catch the Picadilly
line to Kings Cross and subsequently the Circle line
to Paddington. My aim was to reach Paddington in
time to catch the 5.30pm train, the Cathedral Express
to Hereford via Worcester. Those were the days of
steam and on this train there were two silver-service
dinner sittings, the last finishing as the train reached
Worcester though it was possible to stay at your table
and continue to use the drinks service. I would get
home by 9pm, thirst quenched and well fed, usually
returning to London on the Sunday afternoon.

After some months I moved away from Sid and
Peggy, who were always arguing. I took full-board
accommodation at No1 Park Avenue South – run by
a lady called Mrs Carter. The avenue is at the bottom
of Muswell Hill which meant that it was not so easy
to get to work. I would catch a 212 bus to Crouch End
and then a 41 which went direct to Archway. I called

it the "snorting 41" on account of the loud gasp this particular type of London bus made whenever the driver changed gear or used the brakes.

At first I shared a room with another lodger called Vic Matheson who worked in an office in the import/export trade at London docks. He was a quiet lad who was very clever at chess. This cost me 17 shillings and 6d (75p) a week and then I had my own room for 21 shillings (£1.10). There were five male lodgers including me. There were trainee vets, students studying at Kings College, trainee architects and from time to time foreign students. One of the architects named David, a tall lad who always wore a tweed jacket, check shirt and tie, had a most unusual hobby. His passion was to plan a weekend trip using only the little-known branch lines, from London to the Lake District area and back for example, sleeping in the station waiting rooms if he was able to. He would use the regional time-tables known as Bradshaw's, the final issue printed in May 1961.

The Beeching report on proposed railway closures was under preparation at the time so David had plenty of scope until the government, acting on Dr Beeching's report, set about closing 6000 miles of track in 1963.

For two weeks we had a Japanese student at the digs called Nomora Nakamichi. He spoke very little English and bowed gratefully whenever he tried to speak. To Mrs Carter's great annoyance he took two, sometimes three, long, hot baths a day but he never understood her concern.

I seemed to be getting along with everybody at work. Mrs Carter was a likeable landlady, easy going and never minded if we brought girlfriends in to stay. She was however sad, having recently lost her husband which necessitated the need for lodgers as a source of income. We bought her flowers from time to time to show our appreciation. At work I became friendly with Alan Millar and George Hunter, both colleagues in the test laboratory.

Alan was a jovial guy and we got on well. He was learning to play the saxophone and knew quite a lot about jazz. He introduced me to the Marquee Club in Oxford Street where Tubby Hayes used to play, and where the Rolling Stones gave their first live performance. Our favourites were the Modern Jazz Quartet (MJQ) whose recordings I still listen to. Alan knew some good Indian and Chinese restaurants and explained the strange menus to me. I hadn't tried these cuisines before and I took to them instantly. As well as this, I was often invited to his house in Walthamstow for an evening meal prepared by his mother who was very kind.

George Hunter was married to Jackie and they lived in a first-floor flat at 46 Beaversbrook Road, Holloway. Both Alan and I were invited to George's flat one evening to meet Jackie, a visit which sparked a routine meeting every Thursday evening. We were introduced to their friends Mary Charters and Heather Welsh who also came along.

Mary was great company and was fluent in cockney rhyming slang. The one I liked was down the frog and toad to the rub-a-dub-dub, which translated as "down the road to the pub". Mary and I went out occasionally and to this day we laugh about our visit to an air display at Farnborough when she was supposed to bring sandwiches but forgot them.

I had never known such warmth and friendliness, something I never thought I would encounter in London when I first came to the city. But, here it all was, a sort of village life within a great metropolis hidden just under the surface of the exhilarating hustle and bustle of Archway.

All of the others thought I looked like Freddie Garrity of the emerging group Freddie and the Dreamers who had great hits with You Were Meant for Me and I'm Telling You Now. Freddie was formerly a milkman. To them I must have appeared just as dippy. I was particularly nervous about everything, a kind of hypertension I could not shake off and I found it difficult to relax and be myself, and I had great difficulty saying the things I wanted to say. Not even a drink helped at this time.

Eventually my work duties meant that I was unable to meet my friends every Thursday. Sometimes I would go with other engineers on short service trips, other times I would be sent on my own to the north and to Scotland. One of these trips was to a customer in the countryside not too far from Selkirk. I stayed for the weekend at this location and during an afternoon walk in the nearby hills saw below a Scotsman dressed in his kilt and tunic playing the bag-pipes. He was walking across the field piping heartily with a long line of cows following him, presumably on their way to the milking parlour.

On another occasion I visited a customer in Silvertown in the East End of London. I recall a large, ground floor building full of Monotype hot-metal composing machines. The machines consisted of a mechanical keyboard integrated into its own small casting foundry. The compositor would type in a line of text and the machine would cast the line from hot molten lead metal, this is how a page of text was then assembled. Each machine had a crucible of molten metal which was drawn off as required and topped up from a solid bar of metal suspended by a chain end-on in the molten pool. The metal was a composition of 65% lead and 35% tin and antimony to give the soft lead hardness when cast into text. There must have been at least 50 of the machines in operation. The general lighting in the factory was dim except for the keyboard area of each machine which was illuminated by a 40W bulb in a dirty metal shade on an angle-poise. The atmosphere was hot and thick with blue haze from the molten lead crucibles. This was not a place to live and work in, and I was glad to leave it. Health and safety?

A visit to the Express newspaper group in Fleet Street showed me how stupid I could be by not considering my own safety at all times. In order to examine a scanning head I walked close to two giant contra-rotating press cylinders which were running at great speed with the paper web roaring through them at about head level. I was inches away when I noticed my tie flapping in the draught close to the rollers – I could have been drawn in by the two cylinders and decapitated in an instant.

Moving away I walked over to a nearby wall and was physically sick. Shaken and ashen white with fear I struggled to regain my composure over a cup of tea provided by one of the press minders in the rest area.

In order to gain access into any of the Fleet Street establishments it was necessary to be a member of a union thus, all Crosfield engineers became members of the white-collar union ASTMS with subscriptions paid by the company. There was a great deal of demarcation of work processes at that time. On one occasion I had to get the assistance of a paper mover to move a large reel of white paper from in front of an equipment cabinet so that I could open the door. The paper mover turned up with his fork-lift truck but refused to move the reel on account of it being white, apparently he was only able to move pink paper. You had to be very much on your toes and follow the rules, or else!

The union's hold over the printing industry was later broken by the concerted efforts of Eddie Shah, Margaret Thatcher and Rupert Murdoch.

When I returned from service trips I looked forward to getting together with my friends on the Thursday evenings. I longed for a flat of my own and I eventually found a bed-sit I could afford in Parolles Road close to Archway. I left Mrs Carter's and moved in as soon as I could. I had a bedroom and a small kitchen fully furnished but soon found that catering for myself was a lonely thing to do so I started to have my weekday evening meal at Andrew's a cafe on the corner of Elthorne Road and Archway Road, along with several other guys.

I didn't have a television in my flat, there was no time for that, since I was seriously into oil painting on board and canvas. It was pretty much "chocolate box" stuff but I enjoyed moving the paint around constructing the elements of the picture and watching it come alive amid the scent of the oils and turpentine substitute. As I painted I always played popular classical music on a record player which Heather had loaned me, music in my collection such as Grieg's Piano Concerto in A Minor, Dvorak's New World Symphony, Tchaikovsky, Mozart, Sibelius and so on. My friends would be the recipients of my paintings and this spurred me on knowing that I would get encouragement and that my efforts would be appreciated.

I attended real life evening classes for a while at the Hornsey College of Art, drawing everything from bowls of fruit to straight-up nudes. Everything seemed perfectly romantic to me but something wasn't right.

The full power of my emotions and my inability to handle them altered my world when I realised I had fallen in love with Heather. There was nothing I could do about it, suddenly to me she became a green-eyed vivacious beauty whom I adored but my feelings were not returned or even acknowledged. The whole non-affair was extremely painful to me and I quickly became humiliated, ashamed and jealous.

Who knows what might have ensued had I the experience and patience to handle the situation in a mature way? Sadly Heather died in 1993 aged 53 from cancer. Mary had located me in Hereford in 1992 and shortly afterwards told me the news that Heather was terminally ill. I was greatly affected, even after all of the intervening years. I telephoned her not knowing what to expect and had a lovely but sad conversation. She told me that she still had the painting I had given her and I felt immensely honoured – at the time it meant everything to me.

Except for the fact that I had given my bedsit to Heather and moved back to Mrs Carter's, I went into denial and tried to cope with a feeling of devastation as best as I could. I chose to end my close relationship with my friends noting that I needed to improve my self-confidence which hitherto had been virtually non-existent and which, for a short while, remained so.

I wanted things to change and they did. I started to drink heavily for one thing, albeit in a controlled way, and I found a new friend in Ralph Handley. Ralph played sport and was into hockey. He had a sunny disposition which I like in people and he also enjoyed a beer. We would go every day for a liquid lunch at The Mother Redcap opposite the factory for a few jars of Charringtons IPA, a very heady, hoppy, beer the very nose of which would be inclined to send you to sleep.

After work we would retire to the Archway Tavern which was on the fork of Highgate Road and Archway Road, where I favoured Watney's Red Barrel, a rather gassy beer, and drink or play pool every evening. From time to time, others would join us and a new circle of friends developed with conversation ranging from the performance of the horses we had picked at lunchtime to future summer holiday plans.

I sought a change at work too, moving to a new job with a new boss named Brian Pells. Brian had been given the task of forming a research and development section for a new product called

Lumitype. He was of medium height, slender, easy going with a special sunny disposition. On one occasion we both turned up for work with an injured right foot (mine was a twisted ankle) both hobbling around with walking sticks which provoked humour and had synergy prospects.

The section was formed on the Third floor of the new Crosfield premises adjacent to the old building.

It was now the middle of 1961 and Lumitype was a completely new approach to typesetting, involving setting text directly onto film (photo-typesetting) which was then developed and used to generate curved printing cylinder plates made of copper using photo-exposure and acid etching techniques.

The French company, *Societé Lumitype*, developed the Lumitype system principles in a cellar during the Nazi occupation of Paris and were now responsible for manufacturing the accurate glass disc carrying the type founts (styles) which the customer had selected from the numerous ones available at that time. The disc would be fitted into the Photo Unit where it would spin at 10 revolutions per second and the selected character exposed onto film in a cassette by a fast Xenon flash light caused to trigger at precisely the right moment. Characters would be assembled in a line across the width of the film directed by a prism which would move in small increments. Different typefaces (styles) would be accessed by repositioning the spinning glass disc and type size selected by adjusting a turret carrying preset magnification lenses.

In addition to the Photo Unit there were two other parts to the system. One was the keyboard unit where the compositor's work emerged in the form of one inch wide eight channel punched paper tape. There was also a keyboard hard copy automatically produced on an IBM golf-ball typewriter. The punched paper tape would be taken to the Control Unit, which would read the instructions and computations feeding them on to the Photo Unit. Computations made sure that a line of text fitted the page without ragged left and right margins by distributing increments surplus space among the normal spaces in the text, a process known as justification.

My task was to develop a system of Tape Merging which would take the keyboard primary tape and a secondary tape carrying corrections, merge them together and produce a third punched paper tape known as the Clean Tape. To do this I was given bench space and a prototype wireman who could connect together my circuit designs.

Ralph was in the section drawing office next to my area with Maurice Tokarski and Bill Pinder, all happy individuals with ready wit and laughter. Maurice also bet on the horses and being next to a telephone, he would ring his bookie during the afternoon and check the status of the runners and bets we had placed during our lunch hour. In this friendly atmosphere I set about my task in earnest and I discovered for the first time in my life that left on my own I could access a creative ability that I never knew I had. This was due, I am sure, to the fact that I was left to get on with development at my own pace with only occasional demonstrations of my prototype to the Chief Engineer, Brian Pells.

There were no transistors or valves involved, indeed the only transistor of fame at that time was the Mullard germanium type OC71, the revolutionary Texas Instruments solid state 74 series silicon logic circuits being a few years away in the future. The components I had to work with were all electro-mechanical relays, indeed the whole Lumitype system was comprised of hundreds of relays energised by massive 24 volt DC supplies. The relays fell into two main types, a multi-contact on-off IBM miniature "open" relay which could have up to twelve poles and a very fast Clare mercury type relay which could operate in a millisecond but which would only work in the upright position due to the fluid nature of the mercury inside the sealed tube.

My development system consisted of a rack of complicated relay switching circuits, two punched paper tape readers and a paper tape punching unit. These were manufactured by the Tally Corporation of Seattle and, once again, were fine examples of American engineering. Electro-mechanical relays were not reliable, and thus the Lumitype system was not perfect. Hitherto, Lumitype customers would manually strip out text errors in the main film using a scalpel and light box for back illumination and then fit a corrected piece of film in its place but they hated doing this because it defeated the whole purpose of the system.

My Tape Merge unit was pressed into production as soon as it was ready and was installed in the Control Unit together with an extra tape reader for the correction tape. Crosfield became an important customer for the Tally Corporation as the company could not produce Lumitype fast enough to supply the print market.

From time to time overseas visitors would arrive at the company to attend courses on the many Crosfield products. One was an Italian named Vittorio Minutelli from Milan. I managed to find accommodation for him at Mrs Carter's and we became good friends. I helped him with his English and he introduced me to Italian food, taking me to the Quo Vadis restaurant in Dean Street, Soho. We drank a flask of Orvieto with our meal and had Cassata for sweet, a dish originating in Sicily which consisted of layers of gelato (Italian ice cream) and candied fruit. His girlfriend Jane came to England in due course, to marry Vittorio, she was very good looking with dark flashing eyes and long black hair. I was best man at their wedding which was a very small affair held at the Italian Catholic Church in the Clerkenwell Road.

My important work on the Tape Merge system took me to *Societé Lumitype* in Paris. On this occasion I went by ferry from Dover to Calais and boarded a train in Calais bound for the Gare du Nord. The new "franc", worth 100 old francs, had been introduced but the currency generally in use was still predominately the old "franc". I had an excellent late lunch of jambon and pommes frites with a half bottle of vin rouge in the dining car on the train and saw old Paris as it was before modernisation, with its many smelly pissoirs and Metro platforms, the air filled with aromas of Gitane and Gauloise cigarettes. The operators at *Societé Lumitype* showed me how they manufactured the glass disc with all the selected type founts on it. It was a laborious procedure consisting of exposing each character in turn onto the glass which had previously been coated with a photographic emulsion. A large room was dedicated for this operation with the disc at one end and the character projector at the other. The disc would be turned in precise increments for each exposure. When the operation was complete the exposed areas of the emulsion on the disc would be cured using ultra-violet light and the unexposed emulsion washed away leaving perfect black character images in symmetry.

Back in London I had noticed two young women in the production department. They were twins Angela and Brenda. Angela had blue eyes and a lovely figure so I summoned up courage to ask her out. The answer was no! I since learned that she thought I was a snob. Sometime later, and undeterred, I tried again, this time I had tickets for the Royal Albert Hall where the 1812 overture, complete with the cannon effects, among other music was being performed. She said yes and so began an on-off relationship which eventually built up to the point where we were going everywhere together and she became my soul mate so much so that we decided to get married in 1964. Brenda, her sister, married Brendan Phelan, the company printed circuit board expert, in 1962 and they left Crosfields in September 1964 when he took up the position of Works Engineer at Cambion, the electronics specialists based in Castleton in Derbyshire.

Angela and I became members of the Mandrake Club in Meard Street in the heart of Soho. It consisted of a series of basements connected together which comprised the band and dancing area, restaurant, bar, and secluded seating booths. It was a kind of jazz club and we considered it our very own speakeasy only with a drinks licence and entertainment way into the early hours.

We were also regular visitors to the Tottenham Royal dance hall where we listened and danced to Ray McVay and his band. I loved to do the Twist and I am transported back to these times whenever I hear Chubby Checker's recording of Let's Twist Again Like We Did Last Summer.

My first real holiday took place in the summer of 1962 when Ralph and I went back-packing to Yugoslavia taking the train from Paris to Zagreb changing at Munich, and then by bus to the port city of Rijeka, in what is now known as West Croatia. We left Rijeka going south along the Adriatic coast by bus aiming to get to Split but stopping off here and there to explore the different towns and villages.

Yugoslavia was still a communist state which was evident to me by the lack of overt advertising signs normally associated with shops and markets in England. There was plenty of beer available similar to lager, called Pivo, and we drank our fill at many al fresco cafes overlooking the blue Adriatic. I sampled the national drink, slivovitz, a clear-coloured plum brandy, but found it very strong and not to my liking. At Split we took the ferry across to the island of Bracz and camped there for a week. Our food mainly consisted of fruit and cheese but it was possible to get steak and chips by walking three miles across the island to the only restaurant. On our return journey we did a little shopping in Split where I bought Angela a silver filigree bracelet, a speciality of the area. In the busy market place all kinds of farm produce were on sale.

Here I saw an event of animal cruelty I will never forget. A rustic lady, presumably a farmer's wife, was selling chickens. One bird in her keep was misbehaving, tending to run off, she caught the bird, snapped its legs in two, and dumped the poor disabled creature back on the table.

We booked passage on a ferry from Split direct to Rijeka setting sale at 10pm. It was a lovely, warm moon-lit night so we stayed on deck and relaxed with a few jars of beer. The islands to port and starboard were dark shapes silhouetted in the moonlight which turned the calm Adriatic into shining quicksilver, the only distraction was the muffled, slow, constant rhythm of the engines deep inside the ship. The three-week holiday starting from London and back cost me less than £40.

In 1962 my dad had to temporarily close his two fish and chip businesses, because of the potato shortages. The potatoes were available but only at the inflated price of £130 per ton. In November of this year the 1963 big freeze started adding further aggravation to the situation. Between November and early March the temperature never rose above freezing anywhere in Britain.

With my work on the Tape Merge project completed I was shifted back into the old building, to a large empty office. My new task was to form a small department to test and repair new and used Tally Corporation paper tape readers and punches but I still had to act as consultant on Tape Merge, a sideshow which took me to Malta twice and Paris once more.

Many things happened in 1963. For this year's summer holiday Ralph and I decided to hitch-hike to Spain. This would be a strenuous trip and we thought to do some preparations and test our fitness in readiness. One weekend we both came to Hereford with loaded rucksacks intending to walk the 24 miles from Hereford to Abergavenny on the Saturday. I was testing a new pair of walking boots which served me well until about halfway when my feet became swollen, sore, hot and blistered. In some agony I walked off the road and sat on the low banks beside the shallow river Monnow. I took my boots off and let my feet dangle in the cold clear fast-flowing water, it was a sheer delight and I felt the discomfort melt away. I walked the rest of the journey to Abergavenny wearing plimsolls which suited me much better, so much for the boots!

At the start of the holiday in Calais we attempted to hitch-hike to Paris separately and meet at Armand Hazak's house in Paris as the first stage. Armand was a *Societé Lumitype* employee and the rendezvous was pre-arranged. That was the last time I saw Ralph until three weeks later when we reported for work on the Monday. We had planned to meet next on the main bridge crossing the river Garrone in Toulouse but he didn't turn up at the prearranged time. However, I had the tent and I continued by train to Portbou on the Spanish Costa Brava and made my way to the l'auberge de jeunesse (youth hostel) where I joined up with a crowd of English people and decided to stay for a few days enjoying drink, plenty of female company, and beach parties, I was fit and as brown as a berry. From Portbou I caught a train south to Barcelona with the intention of exploring the city for a few days and then I caught a train north again to Figueras in the Girona province of Catalonia. At Figueras I caught a bus to Rosas on the Costa Brava for the rest of my stay. There were no high-rise hotels at that time and I pitched my tent in a camp site next to the beach. My neighbours in the next tent were a Dutch couple who had travelled down on their motorbike. I was to have dealings in Holland in due course and I have to say the Dutch are a lovely people and tend to speak English fluently. My diet in Rosas consisted of peaches, cheese, bread, beer and coffee. I was able to keep in touch with events at home by reading an airmail version of the Daily Telegraph which was available at a price. I would read the paper and drink coffee in the morning sunshine sat at a cafe table on a wooden jetty which reached out a short way from the clean sandy shore into the clear, shallow, sparkling sea.

At night the beach was patrolled by armed Spanish guards, with rifle bayonets fixed, in olive green uniforms and glossy black tricorn hats for these were the days of the Generalissimo. Cavorting in skimpy swimwear was an offence and punishable.

When I went into work on the Monday I was informed that I had to go to Malta that very afternoon. A Lumitype machine was being shipped in a two-engine Bristol Freighter aircraft from Gatwick and I had to go with it. The plane had a crew of three and I was the only passenger which was OK except that I never saw them as they were on the flight deck above the fuselage. I was on my own, the Lumitype system was chained to the floor and there was a pair of seats also bolted to the floor near a window for me. It was a ten-hour trip which included a stop in Nice. In-flight food consisted of a large cardboard box containing loaves of bread, butter, salad, tomatoes, cheese slices and cutlery. I was told to help myself.

When the plane landed in Malta in the morning, dignitaries and the press were at the airport to see the arrival of the new equipment for it heralded more jobs for the inhabitants. The customer, an English company with premises in a suburb of Valletta, had a simple business idea. Manuscripts, sent from all parts of the world, would be photo-typeset and the film posted back to the sender in a matter of days. The staff consisted of dozens and dozens of young Maltese men and women who were very well educated and affordable. My job was to commission the Tape Merge which took about two weeks and I then flew back to the UK on an Air France Caravelle buying my duty free 200 cigarette allowance on board.

When I arrived back at my digs Mrs Carter told me that my mother had been on the phone frantic with worry as we hadn't spoken for over eight weeks. On August 8 the £2.6m great train robbery had taken place and she thought that I might have been involved in it which indicated to me just how remote my existence in London was to her and the rest of my family.

Early in 1964 I flew back to Malta to the same company for more commissioning. This time the aircraft was a BOAC Comet flown by pilots wearing the traditional full-blown BOAC moustache. It was normal to dress formally when flying in these days and if you were a smoker, to step off the aircraft clutching cartons of smart Benson and Hedges gold filters with the prestigious Royal Warrant on the lid of each packet.

During this visit the Casino on Dragonara Point, in St Julian's, was opened much to the anger of the religious community who claimed that peasant people were attracted to the games and were spending their meagre income. When not working I went to Tigne Bay seafront, part of the Sliema area, for a swim. The seafront consisted of a rocky outcrop on which to spread your towel before swimming out to an anchored raft with diving boards. During one swim I found myself alongside a family of seahorses which immediately began to change colour from gold to red when they saw me. Apparently they change colour in certain circumstances so perhaps they didn't like what they saw.

Later in 1964 Crosfields sent me to Seattle to visit the Tally Corporation to learn more about their paper tape readers and punches. Without prior agreement with Tally, my management had ordered 150 Chinese copies of the American designs and it was my task to get them assembled and tested in my new department, a task which I guessed would be fraught with problems. With this in mind I would have to absorb as much information as I could during my two-week visit.

I was booked to fly out on a Pan Am Boeing 707 direct from Heathrow to Seattle using the newly opened polar route. Walking to the aircraft across the tarmac from the departure lounge it seemed to me that the tips of the wings of the craft were almost touching the ground and I guessed that this was because the plane was fully loaded with fuel. Over the Irish Sea, when we had reached 30,000ft or so, the wings appeared to be swept back and uplifted, a beautiful sight which I believed was due to the inbuilt elasticity in the airframe.

This ship was flying home to Seattle where it was built at the enormous Boeing aircraft facility.

There were not many people on board, most seemed to be diamond traders from Holland. Half way through the journey everyone started to walk around and mingle. There was help-yourself hot coffee and alcoholic drinks on a counter at the rear of the plane which was paid for by American or British coinage tossed into a cash bowl also on the counter. At one point the pilot joined the group for a coffee and a chat, it was most informal and typically American.

Seattle, in north-west of the USA in the state of Washington, is known as the evergreen state because of its abundance of pine trees, obvious to me when the cabin doors were opened due to an inrush of a refreshing scent of pine. I was met at the airport by my "minder" Dan who was to look after me during my stay.

Dan was a big man formally dressed with suit and tie and with a short, typically American, haircut. My hair by comparison was long and typical of British styles which tended to follow the Beatles and caused some comment. Dan was a helicopter pilot in the National Guard and on the first Sunday he flew me out to see Jim another Tally employee, the Chief Engineer, who lived with his family in a large house in acres of land surrounded by forest north west of the city. After Sunday lunch Jim drove me to see a gold-rush ghost town called Monte Cristo. We followed snow-clad roads up into the forested hills of Snohomish County and then tried our luck panning for gold in the tributaries of the Sauk river known to have a history of yields. I came away with a few tiny specks of gold in a jar – I still have them!

At the time Seattle was famous for its monorail which runs a mile from the fairgrounds near the Space Needle to downtown Seattle, and also for its 605ft Space Needle with the revolving restaurant on top. Both were star attractions of the World Fair which was held in the city the previous year. The Space Needle was also featured in the Elvis Presley film, *It Happened at the World's Fair*, released in 1963.

My accommodation was in a motel which had a double bed that vibrated for ten minutes if you put a dime in the slot meter on the wall by the headboard. Every day the en-suite bathroom would be cleaned and certified by a blue crepe paper bow fitted around the toilet bowl which read "Sanitized by Acme Services".

At the Tally factory I saw American engineering in action. Many operations were sub-contracted and all component parts were given a thorough check for quality when they arrived at the Goods Inwards Department. Mechanical components were checked for good fit using "go" and "no-go" jigs and were rejected if they failed. The drive mechanisms used small friction clutches which were checked one in every batch of ten. Clutch escapement was controlled by miniature electromagnetic coil and armature assemblies which were tested 100%.

The units were assembled on a production line in a very clean environment with every process well documented. As each unit came off the line it was inspected in the Quality Assurance department and then tested for two days using special test tapes. I was allowed access to all of the drawings and specifications and copies were freely given. To help me in my endeavour, the company also gave me a complete kit of small tools needed for assembly and alignment.

One component set I was not privy to was the punch block and punch pins used in the punched paper tape generator. These were made from hardened tool steel carefully manufactured and honed so that the pins fitted the block perfectly. The quality of these needed to be such that hundreds of thousands of holes could be punched in paper tape without undue wear. To aid the punching action, the paper was lightly oiled which gave rise to "chads", the waste after-punch, which unless carefully contained appeared everywhere and stuck to everything.

Later on, after much head scratching, it was conceded that the Crosfield "Chinese" punch block and pins would never work and recourse was made to the purchase of the American made parts, the manufacture of which remained a jealously guarded secret by the Tally Corporation.

My two weeks with the company soon passed and I made my way back to the UK stopping off in

New York for the final weekend, to try to retrace some of my father's footsteps evident in his photographs from twenty years earlier. I visited the Empire State Building, Times Square, Jack Dempsey's Restaurant and I saw the newly released film Whatever Happened to Baby Jane, starring Bette Davis, on Broadway.

In the spring of 1964, Angela and I got married and moved into a furnished, ground- floor flat in Ferme Park Road off Crouch End. By the end of the year we were a family when Angela gave birth to my son Colin. I considered that my new status as a father meant that we needed a house.

I was all but finished with London anyway so I set about finding another job with new horizons.

Chapter 5

Breakdown and Recovery

I had finished with London and by the end of 1964 I had taken a job with the Plessey Company. This, I calculated, would mean that I would be able to get a house and a mortgage easily because I would be working for a major company which had blue-ribbon prospects, an important factor in those days.

Our destination was to be Poole in Dorset but the factory premises there would not be ready until the spring of 1965 so until then I would be working at Plessey premises in Havant where a new team was being formed.

For the time being we moved into a vacant holiday bungalow on the sea front of Hayling Island which I quickly nick-named "devil's island" due to the high winds and high seas. These conditions were perpetual during the winter months we stayed there but at least I was able to claim accommodation and bus fare expenses from the company. While living there we were able to receive on WRL, *Wonderful Radio London*, the new pirate radio ship anchored off the south coast which had opened up in time for Christmas.

To lift our spirits we began looking for a suitable house in or near Poole. We had to choose something affordable yet we wanted something with appeal.

We finally settled on a bungalow in Corfe Mullen. It was a half-hour bus ride to Poole centre but only ten minutes down the road to the new Plessey factory. The price for the bungalow was £3,500 which was quite a lot for us at that time. It was built in 1963 and had two bedrooms, a large lounge, nice kitchen and bathroom. Rendered on the outside in white with window frames painted a pale blue, it had the name of Sirius, the brightest star in the night sky, moulded in iron rod and also painted blue, fitted to the right-hand side of the front door. There was a large front garden with fir trees and the rear garden included the garage which was approached along a sloping drive. This was 12 Hilltop Road where we would live for the next six years

Working for Plessey was going to be very different from working for Crosfields in London. I was to go into the development laboratory where all my colleagues had university degrees or HND, higher national diplomas. They were all clever, able, individuals who soon found out that I was not in their class and I began to feel inferior.

My first task was to get to know the established electronics technology called "logic" which is based on circuits having only two states, either ON or OFF with counting systems based upon binary mathematics. It all sounds technical and it was. Furthermore, I didn't understand any of it and no-one would help me. At first the company designed their own logic cards which had multiple circuits using normal transistors and other components. I used these to build a prototype Magnetic Ink Character Recognition reader.

On every cheque, even today, there are characters printed along the bottom of the cheque in magnetic ink. There are only 13 characters used and it is known as the E13B fount. When cheque counting, each cheque passes through a magnetic force to magnetise each character. Then, passing at speed through a scanning head, the cheque identity can be recorded because of the unique pattern of the detected electronic pulses.

Using the logic cards I got this to work and so far I felt I was holding my own. It was very interesting and I developed the system step by step, learning as I went along.

There were several projects like this. Soon the old logic cards gave way to the 74-series integrated circuit chips from Texas Instruments in the USA. At first these were in short supply but eventually became plentiful, in all kinds of models, heralding a quantum leap in design possibilities. I was beginning to feel that I could not cope and pondered on a way out.

Poole had a great harbour with several good drinking dens on the front. One of these , the Sloop, had a parrot which would swear loudly for no reason at all and had to spend long periods covered up to keep it quiet. It was in these places that I loved to drink my beer and generally get a good feeling about myself even though behind it all I knew a crisis was looming.

I guess my bosses, realising that I couldn't cope, suggested that I should transfer to the test department where they were testing American "Bunker Ramo" machine tool products which were being made by Plessey under licence. I had to take the post but felt demeaned. Now I would have someone chasing me for results and I was no longer a free-thinker. On the positive side I had first-hand experience of logic, the new 74-series in action, but I had this strong feeling of going nowhere. I was determined to leave and find other employment.

On October 21 1966 I came home from work to see on our black and white television dreadful pictures of the Aberfan disaster in Wales where mostly young children, 144 in all, were killed when a National Coal Board tip slid away after torrential rain and enveloped the school below in black slurry. It was possible to have given a warning but the emergency telephone line from the tip site to the town had been vandalised. The children were on their last day of term and looking forward to their holidays.

Shortly after this disaster I embarked on a mini-disaster of my own. I decided that I would leave Plessey and join a technical publishing company called *Technical Pages* who sent me to Marconi in Chelmsford Essex, to be interviewed by the established technical writing team. I passed all of the checks. The option given was for me to move to Marconi and work as a sub-contracted technical author, or, for me to work partly from home and partly from the TPL offices in Portsmouth. Angela and I considered the move to Essex and we even saw a lovely house in Maldon which we could afford, but we chose to stay where we were and invoke option two.

In July 1968 my daughter Michelle was born. She was so lovely with a shock of golden hair. I owed my family everything and I decided at this stage I would somehow find a slot for myself where we could all be happy and I would earn really good money – being self employed seemed to be the only answer and I was beginning to get the urge to consider something of the kind.

I didn't have a car and was travelling around quite a lot by train and bus visiting Marconi, going to the Portsmouth office, and then back home, once a week, sometimes twice each week. I smoked heavily and drank far too much dreaming of the future that could be mine. The project I was working on was writing manuals for a Saudi Arabian radar system which Marconi was about to deliver. It wasn't difficult but the whole venture was cut short when I became ill.

My first symptoms were acute paranoia, thinking my telephone line was tapped and my movements being monitored. My sense of smell went awry and then I went off my food. The lovely dinners Angela served up smelt dreadful, everything smelt dreadful. Fortunately I had some insight so all of these notions were as real to me as anything could be and I started to try to outwit these unknown demons by taking evasive actions such as constantly looking over my shoulder when I went out and being mindful of the telephone which was red, which didn't help either.

Pretty soon I was diagnosed with a nervous breakdown, causing schizophrenia with paranoia and for my family's safety I was admitted into Herrison Hospital in Dorset. I was shown into a ward where I started to pace rapidly up and down in the corridor feeling greatly confused, helpless, and with what seemed like the weight of the world on my shoulders. No-one was taking any notice of me, that is, until about two hours later when I collapsed on the floor. Just then, everything seemed to click into operation. Two doctors appeared as if from nowhere, I was quickly examined, given oxygen, and then an injection which put me into a blissful sleep.

It was morning when I came to, and for a few moments I felt refreshed. The feeling was short-lived however when the demons started to flood back into my mind. I couldn't reason anything out, wouldn't eat, and was even suspicious of the doctors. I felt immensely vulnerable. My medication routine involved taking 200mg of largactil three times a day. I wasn't used to these pills and they immediately put me into a drowsy state of mind. I was conscious throughout the day but only just. I remember laughing inwardly to myself about my predicament, wondering if the pills were really lager pills! – it wasn't a laughing matter of course because I knew that when I got better, if I got better, I wouldn't be able to continue with my employment.

This ability I had, to hold on to personal awareness, is what I took to be "insight" which was fortunate because some ill patients, I learned, do not have it.

During the course of a month I began to get better and more self assured. Slowly I began to see everything around me in a different light, it was as if I had been away for a long while and had just returned home, and my memory and ability to evaluate my situation, began to return. Much of the time I had been sedated and spent most of it dozing in an armchair.

Angela came to see me as often as she could. I was allowed out of the ward and we went for a walk and sat in the garden. Seeing her was a tonic for me. She told me everything was OK at home though she had had problems withdrawing our money from the bank over some technicality. Angela told me that my employers, TPL, had terminated my employment in a straightforward manner but had given me some severance money which we gratefully received.

I longed to get home and four weeks later the day arrived when I was released, deemed fit to go back into circulation once more. Clutching my bag and medication prescription I stepped into a hospital car and was driven back to Corfe Mullen. I arrived home feeling and looking like a beaten-up rodent with considerable weight loss. Once again I had the feeling of having been away for years, never mind a month, but, I had returned.

To begin with I didn't try to think about the future and employment prospect rather, I tried to take matters in my stride suspecting that I was not fully recovered. I had agoraphobia as a by-product of my illness and a fear of travelling on the bus. All of this led to unwanted anxiety but it did eventually subside.

So back to work in some shape or form. Who on earth would want me, and offer me sanctuary? I considered everything from cleaning cars to being a postman but left out employment as a bar tender! These were the sort of jobs where I thought I would not require excessive brain work but was I underestimating my ability?

I put my pride to one side and telephoned the personnel department at Plessey, my original employer, to see if they had a vacancy. I told them about my situation, that I had been ill for quite a long time, and left it at that. A day or so later I received a call asking me to go down to the factory. They had a vacancy in the Test Equipment Design Department and I was to be interviewed by the department head. The outcome was that I got the job. It was a free-thinking job which suited me. There were objectives to meet but certainly no main-stream pressure. The job involved designing test equipment and it suited me very well.

I thought my way through many projects learning as I went along and using more and more new devices in my designs. I found, however, that I had to think very hard about everything I did and discharge my time at work and outside work in a logical and sequential way relying on lists to see me through. I was aware of this trait of mine and I put it down to my illness and the effect of working through the medication which I had to have every day. Unfortunately, there was another trait which was not nearly so creative. This was the inherent side effect of forgetting everything I had done within two weeks of doing it. Fortunately all my designs at work were recorded onto drawings.

In 1969 Angela and I took Colin and Michelle for a holiday in Ireland. We travelled by air to Dublin and then by coach to Wicklow, to stay with Angela's mother. During our stay I went with Angela's brother Bill to catch trout for tea. This he did by knowing where they were lying in the stream, outpouring to the beach, and tickling them. When the moment was right he would scoop them out of the water. In a matter of an hour he had caught ten good-size fish which we had fried with a little butter and flour. They were delicious and a treat I shall never forget.

Sadly during this holiday I had another breakdown and became severely stressed. It was as if I had switched from a normal state into one of blind panic. We had to leave as soon possible and try to get home quickly. Angela had to deal with me and the children while at the same time I wrestled with the arrangements as best as I could. We reached Dublin airport at 11am on the Wednesday only to be told that the aircraft we were to catch had been delayed by six hours. I was in a very distressed state but eventually we took off and by 10pm we were in Birmingham. Somehow we found a small hotel which would take us for the night but I wasn't well and didn't really sleep. Fortunately Angela and the children did. Next morning we went to the Birmingham Royal hospital and found a doctor who arranged for me to have a sedative and a small supply of medication which I took immediately.

Clearly I had tried to do too much and wasn't up to it. We spent the rest of the day travelling by train from Birmingham New Street to Bournemouth and subsequently to Poole, catching a taxi to take us the rest of the way.

Next day I was taken into Herrison hospital again but this time to a new open wing which had doors without locks and lovely gardens. Here I stayed for two weeks while I recovered. Among the patients I remember was a chap called James. He was supposed to be resting after a bout of over-activity. But, what charmed me was his hobby. From a small personal case he carried, he would take out all of the components he needed to make fishing flies. He withdrew a small vice, intricate tools, hooks, twine, and a variety of multi-coloured feathers. With the vice suctioned to the table he constructed the most beautiful lures I have ever seen. I was sure no fish would be able to resist them. He told me he loved fly fishing but was anxious to get better and go back to his family.

Back at work again I settled down and continued to design test equipment. A year later I was offered a post in the memory systems department as a test engineer. What was attractive was the fact that the department was moving to Towcester in Northamptonshire. If I accepted the post I would have the chance to get a three-bedroom house as part of the relocation package. I discussed the offer with Angela and we decided to go for it.

By this time house prices had increased. I managed to sell the bungalow for £6500 and then bought a new linked-detached house for £10,000 situated on an estate not far from the new Plessey factory in Water Lane. The department move had yet to take place and our new house was not yet ready when we had to vacate the bungalow after a quick sale. Generous relocation expenses paid for our accommodation in a flat in Bournemouth while events sorted themselves out.

Shortly after we settled in Bournemouth Colin contracted an infection from food poisoning and had to go into isolation in Bournemouth hospital for two weeks. He recovered completely and soon afterwards the department I now worked for moved lock, stock, and barrel to the new factory in Towcester.

We moved too, to a hotel in the town, where we continued to live out of suitcases because our new house was not yet ready. Our problems multiplied when, first Michelle, and then Colin, caught measles and we were asked to leave the hotel. The matter was solved when my parents agreed to have the children in Hereford.

Eventually our house was ready and we moved in. It had been completed to a very high standard and we were so pleased to be in our own home at last and to have the extra space and the additional room.

My work involved testing a new type of data storage system based on the technology known as "plated wire". At the time it was a system with the fastest access-time available, in that data could be retrieved and rewritten in a 250 microsecond cycle. It worked by using plated wires threaded through copper track loops on a circuit board. Using electronics the wire at each intersection, a "bit", could be made to memorize a magnetic condition which could be detected and altered at will. The boards were large and there were many of them. We called the whole arrangement "the stack".

The only integrated circuits capable of working at this speed were known as "ECL", emitter-coupled-logic, devices. These were non-saturated circuits which consumed a great deal of power.

There were several test engineers. At first it was necessary to get the memory system, known as the S250, to work and then to test it at high and low temperatures in large environment chambers. For this reason there were duffle coats to wear when testing at -15 deg C and salt tablets, and water to drink, when testing at + 30 deg C. The periods spent in the chambers could be quite lengthy and run into days.

Work patterns often involved night shifts starting at 10pm. I used to like the night shift and the challenge of getting the system fully tested by the time the management arrived for work at the break of day.

My house was not far from the factory and I could walk the distance easily or get a lift from one of the neighbours, I didn't have a car and couldn't drive.

Early In 1975 I had another breakdown and tried to get help from the Samaritans. I wrote down a comprehensive list of all of the symptoms I was experiencing such as depression, feelings of hopelessness, a tendency to cry and worthlessness, and went to see a doctor at Northampton hospital who asked if he could keep the list. He prescribed a course of three ECT's, electro-convulsive therapy, the first treatment to begin the next week.

This day-treatment starts with a general anaesthetic and next minute you are awake. When I came to, there was a strong smell of ozone but I couldn't relate to anything. I was just me, with no memory or thoughts of any kind. I was offered a cup of tea and guided to a seat by the window overlooking a garden. After a while my self-awareness returned and I can only describe my head as being freshly tuned and alert. When I was ready a hospital car was provided to take me home.

The following week I had the second course of treatment but declined to go for the third due on the week after that. From this time onwards my outlook changed. I immediately fixed up driving lessons for myself and bought a second-hand Vauxhall. I began to view my life, and expectations, with a renewed realism and the depressive condition I had melted away.

I hated my 8am 'till 5pm work regime and decided to take my fortunes into my own hands, the ECT treatments I had had made me bold. There had to be a better life for me and I was determined to seek it out. So, during spring 1976 I gave in my notice to my employers, found a job and a house in Hereford and let my Towcester dwelling to an American family from the local USAF base.

My new employers were Baugh and Weedon Ltd, a small company engaged in the design and manufacturing of NDT, non-destructive testing, equipment. B&W was a well-run company with a sophisticated range of equipment and recognised as market leaders in their field. The equipment took many forms but mostly worked by injecting a pulse of energy into the metal object under test, such as a welded pipe to check for a secure weld, and reading the profile of the returned signal. It was fascinating technology and I wished that I could play a useful part.

It didn't turn out like that however and I seemed to have jumped out of the frying pan into the fire and in 1977, after 18 months, I gave in my notice and was on the move again. I was seriously running out of credibility and I knew it.

My next job involved travelling to Malvern everyday but I fared no better. In the new year of 1979, due to a drop in orders and a cancellation, I was made redundant.

My brother David had emigrated to Australia in 1974 and in April 1978 he married Cheryl. He had gained a BA in Political Sciences at the Australian Nation University and was in secure employment working for the Australian Civil Service. Whereas I, by comparison, had been chasing an illusion, a dream, trying to find that special personal space which was denied to me, and, now, I was all washed up.

But could it be that out of all of this chaos, a guardian angel might be watching over me, could it be that I had taken the long path to get to where I needed to be and salvation was just around the corner?

Chapter 6

Self-Employed

It was April 1977 and here I was at the age of 39 with a young family, no job, and no job prospects. Yet, I had been given the greatest gift of all, my freedom. It was a surreal situation and it made me laugh. Everyone I knew or had known relied upon a job but this wasn't for me any more, as far as I was concerned. I had broken the mould and I was relieved to get shot of the notion of working for someone else. I would now rely on the dormant creative spirit which I knew I had but which, due to poor communication skills, I seemed only to be able to use on rare occasions.

Now I would have to train this spirit to come to the forefront and start to work for me and start solving problems. The need was immediate.

It was difficult to shake off the gravity of my situation at first but I lost no time in procuring an A0 drawing board and building a light box. The light box consisted of a large wooden frame fitted with ¼ inch thick, tough plate glass supplied by Spinks of Hereford. The glass was supplied frosted on the underside to disperse and diffuse the back-lighting evenly from the strip lights I had fitted inside the box. In due course I would spend many happy hours using these two pieces of equipment: the board for mechanical and electronic drawings and the light box for printed circuit board artwork.

Luckily my house, which was built in 1907 and was the designated Station Master's house, had many rooms with tall ceilings and I turned the front bedroom on the first floor into my studio. It had large bay windows and panoramic views across Hereford rooftops with the cathedral and church steeples of All Saints, St Peters and St Martins clearly visible. I had the walls and ceiling stripped and repapered with a simple anaglypta which was then painted in brilliant matt white.

Terry Bowley did this work for me to a high standard. I had a gas fire fitted, a desk, filing cabinet and telephone extension installed and I was ready to go. It was going to be a wonderful place to work from, a room filled with light and optimism.

One of the first important work contracts I negotiated was with Racal of Tewkesbury, for the design of a complete unit. Racal were sub-contractors to the Ministry of Defence and with the Northern Ireland troubles going on at the time I guessed that this unit was one of a suite of units which together made up a system used for locating the source of radio transmissions. The circuitry for my unit had already been designed by Racal and I had to package everything, manufacture and supply a prototype. The quality had to be of military standard and the unit finished in drab olive green. The contract was worth £2000.

I realised soon enough that I needed money to live on and to pay for the ongoing costs of my projects. At first I did not know when I would get paid. Certainly I could only invoice for my money when the job was completed and then Racal may not send me my cheque for six weeks after that. This turned out to be the norm for all contracts so at the outset I needed money to tide me over. Cash flow, as with all start-up businesses, was a problem.

There were two options. One was to go to the bank and the other was to appeal to Social Security. I went along to the unemployment office and explained my predicament. They were very good and allowed me to sign on for eight weeks. I said that I would repay the money as soon as I had cash flow and I was duly registered as a JCB driver looking for work.

Later, when I tried to repay the money, they told me there was no mechanism which would allow me to do this. They wished me well and I was signed off.

The bank option was a different matter altogether. I had an account with the Midland Bank in High Town and I went along to see the manager. I told him about my plans and asked for a loan of £500. After I had finished explaining myself, to my astonishment, he grudgingly sanctioned the loan but then proceeded to tell me to get back to work when I had spent it!

I needed this banker's form of compassion like a hole in the head. I told my wife Angela about the affair and next day she went to the bank and demanded to see the manager. She obtained the interview and let fly like a wild cat at him for taking liberties and speaking discourteously to me. When provoked, Angela could reduce such a person to a red-faced dummy and I loved her for it.

A few months later I returned to the bank to repay the loan. At the counter I was told that the manager would like to see me and I was ushered immediately into his office. With the offer of a cup of coffee he proceeded to enquire how things were going. I was full of optimism and liked to talk about my endeavours so we chatted for some while. After another shaking of hands I departed and headed across the road to Barclays Bank where I opened a new account and transferred all my Midland account funds into it.

To an outsider it must have been confusing for it would have appeared that I had no job at all but I nevertheless appeared to be surviving. This was due to the fact that I chose to keep myself to myself and my affairs totally private. I would start work at 9.30am, continue until 1pm, and then take a working lunch usually finishing for the day at 4pm. I was totally focused on my work load and my customer needs.

Sometimes delivery requirements meant that weekend working was involved too, I would never entertain any thought of letting them down. Sometimes I suddenly became very tired when working. The simple process of lying stretched out on the studio floor and drifting into sleep for ten minutes or so always corrected this and I would resume work refreshed.

Such small events like this, which you could not do if you were working for someone else, helped to make me very efficient. "Small is beautiful" and I relished every moment of every day. There was space and time for beer-benders too which I viewed as a celebratory reward for my challenging new-found independence and prospects.

In the new year of 1980 I was offered the opportunity to go to Libya on a one-month contract on an all-found basis for a tax free sum of £1000. I had to sign up with a company called Lane Parson which had contracts looking after the communications requirements of the Libyan government. Alcohol was forbidden in Libya and I wondered if I could do without a drink for that length of time.

I flew from Heathrow to Tripoli on the scheduled British Caledonian DC-10 flight otherwise known as the flying beer barrel by the thirsty oil men who worked in the oilfields in the Libyan desert. As it turned out the people I stayed with, a New Zealand family, brewed their own beer behind doors using compressed ingredients and hops brought into the country in the form of brickettes disguised as bath-time herbal remedies. Customs officers examined everything at the airport confiscating any clothing with a Marks and Spencer label and removing anything with sexual content such as newspapers with page-three girls.

My place of work was a secret police station compound behind high walls on the outskirts of Tripoli. There were prowl cars and a large radio transmitting station which was part of the national police radio link. I was allowed to use the link to talk to my counterpart in Benghazi to discuss technical problems and sometimes just for a chat. I was on my own except for occasional visits by Pip my New Zealand minder. He spoke Arabic and told me that the Arabic name of the station chief translated into Mr Keys.

Pip was a dynamic and clever engineer. One night there was an enormous storm and when we arrived at the station in the morning we found that lightning strikes had all but destroyed the transmitter. He systematically worked his way through the damage and together we had the equipment back on the air within four hours. The Libyan police were adamant that this was the work of the Israelis.

In the station workshop I would be busy servicing faulty American UHF multi-channel transmitters and receivers, the same type of equipment I had worked with at RAF Henlow years earlier. The problems with the transmitters were the same too, deteriorated insulating blocks blown by the radio frequency power when the equipment was turned on.

Spares didn't seem to be a problem and I wondered how such equipment got into the hands of the Libyans in the first place – despite sanctions? I guessed Lane Parson knew the answer. As I worked I could listen to the BBC World Service on a communications receiver. I remember listening to Terry Wogan as he introduced the Genesis hit Follow Me, Follow You, a tune I thought had a trace of Arabic music and which carries me back to that time and place whenever I hear it.

The Libyans had a wonderful legacy left by the Italian ex-pats who were expelled by Gaddafi in 1970. This was the ability to produce excellent bread, pastries and cakes. In Tripoli there were decked-out bars and restaurants which in the days of King Idris and the Italians once sold alcoholic drinks. Where the optics and rows of spirit bottles would have been there were now disappointing bottles of Seven-Up and Fanta Orange on the back-lit glass shelves behind the counter. However, it was in one of these restaurants that I had a lovely meal of deep fried calamari and french fries but the Seven-Up I bought had pieces of cardboard floating in it.

Back at the station they provided me with delicious sandwiches for lunch but I was also allowed to pick oranges from the trees in the grove next door entered by a metal door in the compound wall. These were the best oranges I have ever tasted and near the end of my stay I thought I would collect a few to take back home. But then I heard on the BBC World Service news that the Palestinians had started to poison Israeli Jaffa oranges with injected mercury, so, with British customs in mind, I thought better of it. It was February 1978.

During my time off, I wandered around Tripoli and saw the port filled with scores of ships of all kinds. Many were busy unloading and many others were anchored offshore waiting for clearance to dock. Libya was rich in oil and importing just about everything. One ship in particular was fitted out with aerials and was in fact a broadcast vessel used to preach propaganda when stationed off the Israeli coast. Unfortunately the Israelis took exception to it and machine gunned it from the air. It was lying at anchor, a blackened hulk which had obviously had a bad time.

In the town, I found the souk and saw several shops which had windows full of gold and silver items such as bracelets, bangles, rings, necklaces and countless amulets. These were genuine treasures simply shovelled into the window space, not neatly arranged as you would see in a British jeweller's shop. The treasures were sold by weight using what appeared to be crude hand-held scales.

Many young Maltese boys and girls came to Libya to work as house boys and maids. Before going back home they would cash in their Libyan Dinars for gold in the souk because they could later trade it for English pounds profitably.

Pip, the New Zealander, had gone into the desert to visit military installations along the Chad border with Libya, ostensibly to survey the communications installations and future requirements. On his return he asked me to review his sketches and make cleaned-up drawings of the ten installations he visited. This consisted of map reference, plan layout, equipment details and operating frequencies. At the time Lane Parson had taken a lease on a down-town, first-floor, room with a view to opening an office.

On my last Friday, a holiday in Libya, I set about my drawings in the so-called office on my own when at about mid-morning, in the street below, hundreds of banner-carrying Libyans marched down the road chanting and waving Gaddafi's little Green Book in the air. They stopped outside the office and held their meeting – I thought for a while they had come to get me since my instructions were to take the roll of finished drawings back to England with me in a few days and hand them over to the intelligence authorities. It was very threatening.

Lane Parson, as a company, was doing very good business in Libya bidding for government contracts for communications equipment and spares. Part of any deal meant entertaining Libyan officials in London. This involved company agents collecting them from the airport in a chauffer-driven limousine, taking them to the best hotels, and supplying girls. Sometimes the girls would stay with officials and accompany them when they wanted to visit the sights of London during the day. At night they could be entertained at any one of the many North African restaurants, some in the neighbourhood of the Libyan Embassy located in Knightsbridge SW1.

I was offered the opportunity to savour some of these delights when I returned to England but I cannot say that I got involved.

After my return from North Africa I continued to win contracts to design printed circuit artworks. Nowadays this is achieved by using precise software packages on a personal computer but at that time my artworks consisted of black crepe tapes laid out on transparent polyester sheets from which photo negatives were produced using an industrial camera. The negatives would be used by the manufacturers to produce the circuit boards.

One day I received a call from an American working at GCHQ in Cheltenham. GCHQ, also known as "The Puzzle Palace", is the secret government communications centre where intercepts are carried out and information disseminated. Apparently there was a need for several large circuit boards to be designed and manufactured urgently. As always, I got the contract because I was willing to put all else aside and start the job immediately. It paid very well.

Some of my work consisted of helping companies to second-source circuit boards and subsequently build their own versions of an existing product much more cheaply. We talked of Chinese copies then, and we still do, but I could see that it was prevalent in the UK at that time as well.

Another interesting task was the work I undertook for a Welsh company whose business was to do with the farming industry. Their products were computer-based and concerned with the management of farm animals, particularly cows. Each cow would wear a belt around its neck which carried a transponder. The transponder didn't carry a battery but relied on using radio energy focused on it, to power a small secondary transmitter which radiated the cow's personal data.

When a cow entered the milking parlour it had to walk through a gate which triggered the cow's transponder and retrieved the beast's personal identification information. The transponder was triggered again when the cow was connected to the milk-collection apparatus. In this way information such as the beast's weight and milk yield was automatically inputted to the computer. Today, security tags on clothing, for example, work in much the same way, when, if you try to leave the store with the widget in place on the item, the store alarm will be activated.

I sorted another contract for myself which took me away from home for one month. This was with Pedigree Pet Foods based at Melton Mowbray, Leicestershire. This company used around three million cans every day and to limit storage space these were delivered lorry load at a time every 30mins from the Metal Box Company.

The drawing office had several tidying-up tasks which would keep me employed for the month. This is work I could cope with so I negotiated a price with the Chief Engineer who kept raising his offer and then he said, "is that enough for you? Do you need any more?" and the deal was done.

The Petfoods production lines were continually altering which provided work for some thirty draftsmen and engineers. The facility was housed in a purpose- built air-conditioned hall. The walls were painted matt white and there were no windows. Typically American, smoking was not allowed and the accent was focused upon work from 8am until 4.30pm with a half-hour for lunch and plenty of overtime which allowed me to work until 7pm. Next door, in the production area, the noise was so terrible that ear-defenders, and the wearing of hard-hats, was mandatory. Everything was very professional with a high work-ethic.

As events progressed I chose Wye Electronics as a trading name and I used to advertise in the "classified ads" section at the rear of a trade newspaper called Electronics Weekly. One day I received a phone call from the Managing Director of a company called Wye Electronics Ltd based in Derbyshire. He was furious that I should be using the name and threatened to get his lawyers on the case. I shrugged my shoulders and carried on anyway, never to hear anything more about it. An amusing thought crossed my mind that I could perhaps change the name to Why Electronics – it was that absurd.

Naturally, with my ever growing list of customers, I would be asked by them to procure circuit boards as well. Because I leaned on the manufacturers, and formed a good relationship, I always got a good deal on price and delivery. This meant that my income was boosted by the simple process of adding a commission. I would take delivery of the parcels, change the labels, and addresses, and deliver to my customer post haste. I never had any complaints and this service, and source of income, expanded.

Angela, my wife, had taken a job with Bulmer's, the cider makers, meanwhile and with me working from home I was able to take her to work and pick her up as well as look after the children and their schooling time-table.

I saved the money I earned and soon there was enough extra to by our first new car. I chose a 1.4 Austin Allegro and paid cash for it. Champagne in colour, it was a good little car but had a small boot space. It had another attribute too, while motoring near Ledbury we ran over a small pot-hole in the road, there was a mechanical "clank" and the engine bonnet flew up in front of the windscreen! No accident ensued however.

With ever growing resources I later traded in the Allegro for a new maroon-coloured Datsun Stanza hatch-back. I had a pick of number plates so I chose TAP123Y which, with my wry sense of humour, suited me very well. A Nissan Bluebird estate followed and a succession of Ford motors.

To acquire work I would track down companies advertising in the media and telephone for an interview trying to arrange to call upon at least two potential customers per day while out travelling. I always tried to get interviews with the chief engineer, chief draughtsman and production manager.

Sometimes all three would agree to see me together and very often coffee was served.

My sales pitch usually started by explaining my strengths and outlining the projects I had had involvement with. There were always tasks which were "on the back-burner" which I could step into and help move forward.

Several of my potential customers would listen to me and often make the comment that they thought I was "chancing my arm" going it alone but I found ample work and I thought there was enough work around for everybody. Most companies were full to capacity, or simply inefficient, and had to put work out to people like me, to meet production requirements. I felt that I was slightly ahead of my time for the work was abundant and richly rewarding. Payments to me were usually made 30 days after submitting my invoice and I never experienced any payment defaults.

For two weeks in the summer of 1981 I had booked a holiday on the P&O Canberra for my family. The Mediterranean cruise started and finished at Southampton and called at Madeira, Palma, Cannes, Malaga, Gibraltar and Vigo, in Portugal, on the way home. We all had a lovely holiday. I favoured the Alice Springs bar situated at the rear of the ship. The bar had floor to ceiling glass windows overlooking the stern of the vessel and was fitted out with wicker tables and chairs. I downed many pints of lager dispensed under pressure at the bar counter from a never-ending source deep within the ship.

The Canberra was built for the P&O–Orient Line and started life as an ocean liner in service between

England and Australia after whose federal capital she was named. The coming of the jet age made the service unprofitable so in 1974 she became a cruise liner until 1997 when she was broken up for scrap. The Canberra had a tonnage of 48,000 tons and was powered by steam turbines which drove electric alternators directly feeding electric propeller motors.

In 1982 the ship was commandeered to serve in the Falklands campaign and carried the Parachute Regiment and the Royal Marines 9000 miles to the islands, and war. She anchored in San Carlos waters to disembark the troops and was largely untouched by the Argentine aircraft which tended to concentrate on the navy frigates and destroyers. Known as the "Great White Whale" she would have been an easy target but if sunk in San Carlos she would have been too big to sink below the waters.

Work availability and opportunities were so good that I rented a lock-up unit from Hereford Council and changed my business name to Hereford Microsystems. This was Unit 4, Twyford Road, Rotherwas Industrial Estate, which is on the south-east side of Hereford, south of the river Wye. The unit was one of a group of six opposite the then, Thorn Lighting factory entrance and to the rear of the Thorn sports and social club where I soon learned that I could get an excellent "beef burger-in-a-bap" for my lunch.

The lock-up unit was some 600 square feet with a toilet, sink and electric hot-water heater. Conscious that the work area should be as clean as possible, I had thermo-plastic tiles laid over the concrete floor to seal it. I then hired a one-ton box van and drove to

Mike and family about to board the Canberra the year before she was pressed into service in the Falklands War.

the Nortek factory in Congleton to buy new factory tables, work benches and seats for on-the-spot cash. After installing the factory furniture, I took delivery of two large A0 professional light boxes with the idea that I could run two artwork projects together enlisting help where necessary. The whole arrangement looked very smart.

With accommodation and small tool kits for up to five employees I was able to take on assembly work. Generally this involved collecting from my customer free-issue parts and building the items by stuffing the components into the circuit boards and soldering the component tags and wires, sometimes testing the product as well.

The types of assembly work I undertook were power supplies for spark erosion systems for a Gloucester company, modules for the Metal Box Company based in Worcester and many thousands of telephone earpiece inserts for the original BT factory based in Abercarn, South Wales. Occasionally I would get a call from a clandestine operation in London to supply quantities of the earpieces modified with a special reed switch mounted into the circuitry. Other assembly work consisted of high frequency radio transceiver modules and air-sea rescue equipment.

Design work often took the form of producing module testing jigs for customers such as Froude Consign in Worcester. Froude manufactured dynamometers, equipment which scientifically applied electronically variable heavy-duty loads to test other manufacturers' large motor and engine products.

The Froude control systems used a myriad of circuit board modules and all had to be tested. For this purpose they bought automatic test equipment and relied upon me to supply interface test jigs for every module. The test jigs are best described as a spring loaded bed-of-nails, or pogosticks, which made connection with different parts of the circuitry on the underside of the module to be tested when it was fitted into place.

Provision of these jigs was very lucrative for there were many types which had to be individually designed and manufactured and then there were many which were recycled to accommodate design changes.

In 1983 Angela left Bulmer's the cider producers and came to work at the unit. I also met and employed Steve Clements for the first time. Steve was a young man who had good "A" level grades from the Sixth Form College and had a deep interest in electronics and the ever-developing personal computer concept. Steve who was 100% reliable was to be instrumental in helping me design and develop new and very original products in the future.

As well as other employees, I was able to give temporary employment to some of the technical officers from BT Madley, the local satellite station, who were on strike at the time! My own future employment at the satellite station was not too far away.

GKN Technology based at Wolverhampton became another customer. They were responsible for testing to destruction vehicle suspensions – usually a cradle of layer-springs. They had big mechanical test sets which repeatedly put a suspension spring under severe stress until it showed signs of fatigue. These mechanical test sets were under the control of computers which would be fed with an "exercise pattern" to exercise the suspension under test. Sometimes a program of data would be used which had previously been collected by driving data-capture vehicles over rough terrain.

I produced many test sets for GKN. On one occasion they required a piece of equipment which had to record the maximum and minimum of a varying voltage and hold the level. This was a very interesting exercise for me which I completed using only analogue circuits. They ordered five of these.

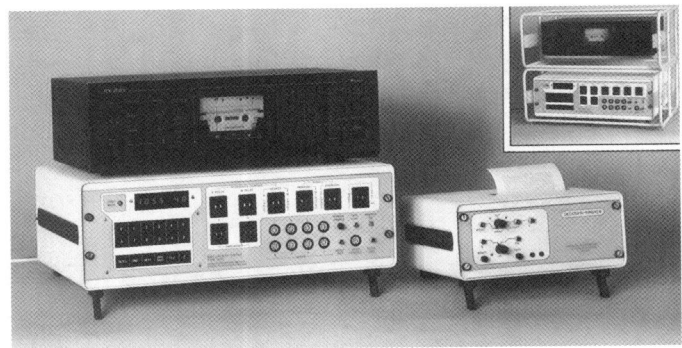

Noise monitor produced for the CEGB.

Nowadays, any worthwhile handheld test multi-meter has these functions as one of its options.

I also had an on-going relationship with the CEGB (Central Electricity Generating Board) research headquarters based in the south of Bristol. My work consisted of designing and building monitoring equipment for evaluating the noise emissions from wind turbine generators. These windmills produce a loud whoosh sound as the blades turn and therefore field test results were needed for planning purposes. High fidelity microphones would be placed at strategic locations near the windmill and in addition, wind speed, wind direction, and humidity would also be recorded. The data, including the sound would be recorded on a Nakamichi professional cassette recorder with the system preset to record only when selected conditions prevailed.

The CEGB has long since been disbanded but at the time their scientific and research headquarters was a beautiful building equipped with the very best personnel comforts. I had many excellent lunches bought for me in their restaurant.

CB radio was quite popular at this time and as a personal exercise I bought two sets and built keying and encoding/decoding system for each one. I placed one at my home in Barrs Court Road and the other at the factory unit across town at Rotherwas. The radios would transmit to each other backwards and forwards across town all day long using codes which I could adjust at will. It was all rather pointless at the end of the day but it did provoke comment from other band users which was interesting to listen to at the time.

Holidays came around every year and in 1983 we chose to take our family on a package holiday to Lloret de Mar on the Costa Brava in Catalonia, northern Spain. There was nothing unusual about this except the method of getting there. We signed up with Travelscene which operated overnight express coach transits from London Victoria to Girona and then used feeder coaches to take us to our hotel.

We left on a Saturday and got to London by train from Hereford leaving at 8am in the morning. The coach was due to leave Victoria coach station at 3pm and we arrived in plenty of time to buy some lunch and for me to stock up with plenty of booze. By this time our youngsters were already feeling tired and we hadn't even started yet. Our bus was a swish double-decker with the name of the travel company in orange and blue displayed in large script across the bodywork. It appeared to be roomy inside but in fact the seats were not comfortable and were designed so that the vehicle could accommodate as many travellers as possible, rather like standard class on an airliner. When the coach departed it was only half full however. We sat together upstairs and had a marvellous view during the course of our journey, particularly notable when we reached Paris at 10pm and wound our way through the city lights on the orbital road.

I did feel sorry for Angela and the children when they became really tired for it was impossible to sleep properly. The night wore on and eventually we reached Girona, at 10am on Sunday. Another hour on the feeder coach and we arrived at our hotel which was a short walk from the beach. Colin and Michelle by this time were wide awake in spite of the night's ordeal and I went with them down to the beach almost immediately. They were elated and had a new found lease of life.

Back in Hereford, two weeks later, after a return trip which was even worse due to delays, I drew up a plan to replace the old rubber electrical wiring throughout the house and make some modifications. One of the structural modifications was to knock down a wooden pantry enclosure so that we could have a fitted kitchen. In the dining room we still had an open fire-place so the wood from the pantry, which was larch, I sawed up for burning. It burned well but would spit out sparks into the hearth. Pinkle, our black cat, was a recipient of the sparks enfilade because she would insist on lying asleep close to the fire. Her fur would singe and she would let out moans of discomfort without waking up until finally we shifted her.

Rewiring the house was a major task but my time was my own so I could take as long as I liked. All of the carpets were removed and also the main floorboards. It was a filthy job with years of dust and dirt rising into the air.

At the time I used to go to the gymnasium at the back of the Merton Hotel called The Factory. I was fitter in those days than I have ever been and fit enough to take on this task. But, at the end of a day's work I was ready for a work-out at the gym and a relaxing soak in the shower afterwards. The rewiring took me a week of physical toil and finally, when completed, a further week of waiting for the new carpets to arrive and be fitted.

Subsequent to the Falklands war Margaret Thatcher's popularity was again on the rise and the country's economy was in fairly good shape. I now noticed a difficulty in obtaining work for it was obvious that businesses were shaking off the old ways and becoming much more efficient and self-sufficient. Sub-contract work, which I had known and relied upon, was becoming non-existent as businesses were modernising and doing everything they needed to do in-house for themselves.

I started to evaluate my position and even questioned the amount of tax I had to pay on one occasion. It was £3000 which was an awful lot of money in those days. My accounts were being sorted by a Hereford company but I learned of a London accountant, Brindley Goldstein who took a fresh look at my books. To my delight they were able to win back the £3000 which was repaid just in time to augment Colin's income while at university. Colin had gone to the London School of Economics in 1984 and graduated in History in 1987. It is well worth listening to, and taking note, of other people's experiences.

With declining work and illness I surrendered the lock-up Unit 4, at Rotherwas. Although I had plenty of money, for I saved as much as I could, I was nevertheless like a fish out of water and adrift. My drinking and the worsening work situation had brought back the old problem of paranoia and I ended up in hospital for a week, ostensibly to "dry out". I was out of kilter and beginning to resign myself to consider being employed again, if someone would have me!

I had been friendly with Don Roberts another radio amateur with the call sign G3FKH. Don was retired and was an ex British Telecom engineering manager who had worked at Madley Satellite Station, a multi-dish receiving and transmitting complex six miles south west of Hereford.

We would often meet for a beer and a chat. Recognising my situation Don suggested that I apply to Madley for employment as they were actively hiring engineers to help with an ongoing expansion programme. Radio amateurs were a preferred species as they had the required radio knowledge and anyway, would fit in well with the indigenous radio amateur community at the station.

I applied for an interview and I turned up at the station clutching a bundle of drawings of devices I had designed hoping to impress the interviewers. The situation was urgent and I needed this job.

It was 1988, little did I know at the time that I was about to enjoy one of the most relaxed work regimes I was ever likely to encounter.

Chapter 7

Employed by British Telecom

Never in my wildest dreams did I think that I would ever find such a secure, bountiful place to work as the British Telecom Satellite Earth Station (SES) at Madley, six miles south west of Hereford city. I joined BT in 1989 and arrived for work on the first Monday of September and immediately sensed the quality of the surroundings, a kind of technical park, and the relaxed pace of business.

After spending some time in the line manager's office receiving an introduction to the company, I was taken to meet my new colleagues and work-mates in the DL section. DL stands for "direct labour" which was the name for a group of engineers who had responsibility to install new equipment for new customer services in the main equipment hall and aerial sub-buildings elsewhere on the 65 acre site. This would be the nature of my job and I was issued with a fine tool kit and personal tool box.

I cannot say that I was received by my new friends with anything more than a strained politeness. They were long-service and time-served after all, and must have taken an exception to an outsider drafted in "off the street" as they saw it. I was older than all of them and they knew I was less qualified on paper. For my part I saw people sitting around and drinking endless cups of tea with a work ethic which seemed to me to be low on their agenda. After a life-time of work-focused endeavour I couldn't help taking exception to it and my feelings surfaced from time to time.

In a short while, it became obvious that the guys didn't like me and consistently found ways to make me feel unwelcome. So I had to consider my position.

I could either have a hard time or an easy time, the choice was clearly mine. Who the hell did I think I was anyway? I chose to have an easy time and one morning when we were all gathered together for a tea break, I apologised openly to everyone for my disposition and changed my outlook completely preferring to drift into the ways of BT and a definitely more harmonious and comfortable existence.

I soon learned that the installation jobs were always completed on time and to a high standard. The skills and knowledge of my colleagues were first class. They had the difficult task of working among equipment which was in service. There was no room for error, or interruption of the services, for BT had a good name to protect and there was always the possibility of compensation due to the customer if his link went down. There was such a lot of equipment local-knowledge to be learned and these guys knew everything.

After a while I was accepted by them and began to enjoy their company and comradeship and they began to trust me. Much of the humour centred on the perceived incompetence of the London-based engineers who were responsible for feeding projects into the department and controlling progress.

Eventually I was introduced to a department "lock in" which usually took place in the afternoon, say, on a Friday. The section door would be locked from the inside and to the casual visitor looking through the window in the door, there would appear to be no-one at home; but in fact, out of sight, the place had become a drinking den. The drinks, paid for, would be spirited in from the bar, in the restaurant area, where one of the DL chaps held jurisdiction.

In the summer of 1990, I was also witness to a DL Bar-B-Q for the first time. The party usually took place on a Sunday, when the weather was expected to be co-operative and there were fewer people around. The team, ostensibly working on overtime rates, would set up the barbecue out of site of the station security cameras behind aerial building No3, to enjoy good food and celebrate the god Bacchus.

All of these liberties ceased with the reformation which occurred before I left the company.

The satellite station exists for the sole purpose of transmitting and receiving signals to all parts of the world using geo-stationary satellites positioned 35,000km above the earth, for 24 hours, 365 days of the year. Madley, built on a WW11 airfield site, opened for business in 1978 but now has 50 satellite antennas in service covering the Indian and Atlantic Ocean regions for international voice, fax data, IP, video conferencing traffic and TV broadcasts. The antenna sizes range from the early Aerial 1 weighing in at 290 tonnes with a 32M diameter dish down to the latest, most efficient, small dish antennas of only 1.8M diameter.

Partial view of Madley Satellite Earth Station.
Printed by kind permission of BT.

Through the magic of Madley, the world was able to learn about the fall of the Berlin wall in 1989, the funeral of Princess Diana in 1997, the Asian tsunami in 2004 and the Beijing Olympics in 2008.

Madley had a sister earth station called Goonhilly built on a 160 acre site on Goonhilly Downs 25 miles from the Lizard in Cornwall. The Downs is a site of Special Scientific Interest. Its natural heath contains 17 of some of the rarest plants to be found in the UK.

Goonhilly station opened in 1962 and immediately took part in the early transatlantic TV broadcasts by tracking Telstar as it passed overhead in low earth orbit. Aerial 1, named Arthur, was used for these early experiments and it is now a listed monument with special scientific interest. Due mainly to the reduction of telephone traffic over satellite links in recent years, BT could not justify having two operational earth stations and Goonhilly closed down in 2008. Its remaining services were transferred to Madley.

It was in this most interesting environment that I began to think about my own projects. At Madley, a week's worth of work could be done in two days leaving time to apply oneself to other things or else shrink from boredom. I would often sit with notebook and pen working out my thoughts into realities, a kind of technical serendipity you might say.

Even though I was now working full time for BT, I kept my business alive as a conduit to exploit possible products that I might develop in my spare time. One such product grew out of my previous association with the CEGB, the Central Electricity Generating Board. They, and the local authorities, were using a device known as the eight-day-bubbler for measuring black particulates in the air and sulphur dioxide gas. The black particulates method interested me and I set out to learn more with a view to automating this part of the overall process. There were no customers in mind, I just knew that if I could design an automatic system, then it was bound to be of interest to someone, somewhere.

The eight-day-bubbler was brought into being by scientists at the Warren Spring Laboratory as a low-cost means of measuring black particulates in the air subsequent to the introduction of the "clean air act" which was passed by parliament in 1956 after the dreadful London smogs of 1952. It was a simple low-cost manual arrangement of chambers which each carried a circular filter paper of a specific type through which outside air would be pumped at a controlled rate. Each day pumping produced a black stain on a filter paper which corresponded to the amount of soot in the air. The sample could vary in colour from light grey to occasionally filthy black. On day eight, a technician would collect the previous seven filter samples replacing them with clean filter papers thereby making the process continuous. Clearly it was labour-intensive.

The filter samples would be measured for degree of blackness using a reflectometer which was first set up using the whiteness of the filter paper as a reference. This "percentage" reading was then entered into a formula to arrive at an assessment of the amount of black smoke pollution for that day.

This was the process which I thought I could automate. This was the latest puzzle I set for myself.

The eight-day bubbler method of monitoring black smoke was adopted by most local authorities in the UK which installed the equipment in city centres where traffic concentrations were heaviest. Its association with smog problems ceased long ago when they became a thing of the past due to the introduction of the clean air act and smokeless fuels. At this time, it was the only method of monitoring black particulates such as those emitted by diesel vehicles in concentrated areas and occasionally, dirty factory chimney stacks. The method was also used by countries on the continent.

The system of measurement was not very accurate but there was a huge data base in existence and I judged that it would never be discontinued in favour of new emerging technologies and I was partly correct as it turned out.

Black particulates, the sort emitted by diesel vehicle exhausts, were thought by clinicians to be the cause of problems such as asthma. Particulates as small as 2.5 microns (a micron being one millionth of a metre) would be able to bypass the human lung defences – a system of cleansing hairs.

The emerging state-of-the-art method for detecting such small particulates was to take an air sample and filter it allowing through only the particulate sizes of interest. The "yield" is captured and weighed using a sensitive micro-balance, a very space-age piece of wizardry.

I should like to mention that I have always held the view that young children wheeled along in push-chairs and prams at pavement level are particularly vulnerable to roadway emissions and should be protected by a canopy fitted with a low-cost air filtration system.

Undeterred by the advance of these modern machines, I continued to build my own black smoke monitor prototype which I labelled the SX100. I developed a system of miniature pneumatics and electronics to control the movement of the various mechanical processes involved. There was only one two-part sample chamber through which reeled filter paper had to pass. It had to open and close when commanded and take a reflection reading of the sample at the end of each timed period which could be preset to be 8, 12 or 24 hours. The reflectometer consisted of an optical sensor and light source fitted inside the chamber.

The precise structure of the mechanism meant that I would need to employ a first-class engineer to machine the miniature parts and fit everything together. I advertised in the Hereford Times using a box

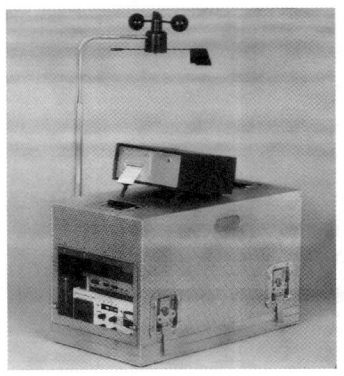

The early SX100

number but there were few replies. One letter passed on to me however had a note inside which simply said "try this number" and gave a phone number. This is how I met Peter Fenn who joined the project working for me from his garage in his spare time.

Peter is a meticulous machinist, designer and fabricator with a world of experience. His interest in, and knowledge of, steam engines was greatly appreciated by me because here was a man who had built a succession of models where everything worked including the tiny pressure gauges inside the cab. He was going to provide just the kind of help I needed. Whenever I visited Peter I was agog at the sight of his saddle-tank shunter engine beautifully finished in metropolitan crimson. On a scale of 1.5 inches to a foot, it was something of a heavyweight model, in contrast to his 4-4-0 American narrow-gauge engines, produced on a smaller scale of 1/20th inch to a foot.

To help me with the microprocessor and associated software involved I had the services of Nigel Prosser, a BT colleague, who wrote the exacting programmes for me. I was greatly impressed and thrilled with progress. However, it would be some time before things started to take off.

To give my part-time business legitimacy I had to have a postal address and somewhere to do development work. I located a 1000 sq ft factory in Peterchurch on the A4348, about six miles west of the Madley satellite station where I worked, on the Old Forge Industrial Estate. Unit 5, was one of eight well-built units built for COSIRA, the Council for Small Industries in Rural Areas, which were intended for letting. Even today not all units are let which is such a pity because they are well-appointed. However, I had special dispensation to take the unit on a short-term let which suited me very well. I bought low-cost kitchen units for benching and moved other equipment in to continue developing the SX100 prototype. I made use of the latest in mobile phone technology and bought a brick-type portable telephone, a Motorola 4800X transportable with a handset, to use at the factory which, as it turned out, was just within range of the repeater. I also organised a telephone answering service which worked well.

Returning to Madley, I applied for a job in the Planning Office and got it. It didn't mean any extra money, or promotion, and I didn't get the job on merit, it was simply that no-one else would take the job. So I moved out of the DL section into an office in the main halls of residence among the managers. My desk was one of two in the office, the other being manned by my boss, a level-1 manager. My duties seemed to consist of compiling lists of wiring schedules on the computer and producing edited pictorial handbooks detailing transmit and receive signal flow charts. I worked closely with the drawing office staff who supported me in my quest to ferret-out information. In doing this, I was not in any shape or form a manager, nor ever likely to be one, but the new post did feel different and working with the drawing office staff was a pleasure.

Managers within BT rotate from job to job quite frequently never staying in one post too long and therefore never having the chance to get embedded. It is an old civil service way of doing things. BT, or the General Post Office (GPO) as it used to be, was at one time very much part of the civil service. These were the days when it took three months to get a residential telephone line installed. Many of the peculiarities of these early times still existed at Madley.

After some months my line manager changed. The new man in my office was Peter Kennedy. He was promoted from DL and I knew him quite well and I liked him. Peter was clever and a first-class guy who cared about the planet and nature. He used to keep a retired donkey in a paddock at his home in Kingsthorne, among other animals.

After Peter, my third level-1 manager was Alan Brookes. Alan came from London and we had something in common, we both liked a few pints. There were several Londoners working at Madley – known colloquially as "01-ers", the old telephone number prefix for London dialling.

We had a lunch break of one hour at Madley and Alan would come with me from time to time, to Peterchurch when I went to collect my mail during this break. There was time to call in at the Broughton Arms for a couple of "swifties" since picking up my mail was a two-minute job. These excursions were very enjoyable until Alan was censured by his manager, a level-2, ostensibly for leading me astray!

Peterchurch has some interesting aspects. St Peter's church held the record for the tallest glass-fibre steeple for some years. The new steeple was the only option left when the original was considered unsafe and too costly to restore to its former glory. Buried in the cemetery are the remains of Private Robert Jones VC. Private Jones belonged to the 716, B-Company of the 24th Regiment and was awarded his VC for his bravery in helping to evacuate the injured from hospital at Rorke's Drift in January 1879 when the enclave consisting of 139 British soldiers was attacked by thousands of Zulu warriors.

Robert Jones didn't die at Rorke's Drift, he committed suicide in September 1898. Because his death was suicide he was not allowed a Christian service on consecrated ground, a strongly held view at that time. However, with due respect to his bravery and his VC, his body was allowed to be passed over the cemetery wall but not through the gate, and, even then, only allowed to be buried non-aligned with the head-to-toe direction of the other burials in the graveyard.

In December 1991 I celebrated my 53rd birthday: a very low-key affair for I was not happy about it. Suddenly it dawned upon me just how old I was. I had reached an age where the outlook for me seemed to be charged with misgivings and in a quiet moment at home I shed a few tears. Then I made myself focus on the saying "tomorrow is the first day of the rest of my life" and I began to feel better about everything.

As a pick-me-up I bought a boat. This was a second hand 24ft GRF (glass reinforced fibre) river cruiser which had four berths, a 20hp Evinrude outboard petrol engine and was remotely steered from the cockpit. She was called Cobra and I moored her at the Upton-Upon-Severn marina. I loved to spend a few days on my own at the marina, from time to time, polishing and painting the woodwork and generally improving, and sometimes replacing, the boat's internal fittings using parts obtained from the local chandlery. Then, with Angela, we made trips up and down the river Severn and to Stratford Upon Avon using the canal system. You really do see so much wild life away from the road lazily drifting with a muffled chugging through the peace and quiet of the countryside at 3mph.

Sometimes we would stay at the marina for a weekend spending time in Upton town making a particular point of being there when the Upton Jazz Festival was in full swing with as many as ten bands playing at different locations in the town and in the nearby meadows. When we were on the boat at our mooring we would often be visited by a particular swan and her three soft grey, good size, cygnets. Knowing we were aboard, she would peck at the side of the boat to let us know she was there and needed to be fed.

At Madley on Wednesday July 1 1992, I was sitting at my desk when the switchboard operator put through a call from my nephew Chris Bush. I was shocked to awkward silence when he told me that my brother Bryan, his dad, had died that morning from a heart attack. I left work immediately to go into Hereford and break the news to my mother and father. At first they wouldn't believe me and at that moment I became a little bit hysterical. They were heartbroken.

Bryan lived in Basingstoke with his second wife Sue. His first wife Lorraine, mother to Chris, and two daughters Denise and Jackie, was now married to Alan Cracknell and living in Hereford. It was Alan who rang me to say that he was taking Lorraine down to Basingstoke to be with the children and he asked if I wanted to come along.

I went but felt I was of little comfort to anyone and seemed in the way. It was generally known that Bryan and I were not very close and this may have had something to do with it. However, I grieved inwardly and felt so helpless towards the others.

The funeral was held a week later at St Andrews in Basingstoke. Sue had arranged for Bryan's favourite Karen Carpenter song *We've Only Just Begun* to be played during the service. Afterwards the funeral cortege wound its way through traffic to the Aldershot Crematorium some 15 miles distant with a slight detour to pass the garden centre where Bryan had been a manager and where the staff gathered outside the main gate to say their last farewell as we passed by.

From this time on I became friendly with Alan Cracknell and I still am. He is a kind good-natured guy with that special sunny disposition which I like so much. Londoners and people from the south-east tend to have this quality and this is the area where Alan hailed from. Now living in Hereford, he is a self-employed window cleaner, but he is more than that. His willingness and reliability has meant that he has been able to carve out for himself a full-time occupation managing all kinds of tasks for his ever-growing network of grateful customers. His only enemy is the weather which can restrict his outdoor work sometimes.

You might wonder what other connection Alan might have with me and my SX100? Alan is a first class driver and has an HGV licence and experience of driving on the continent. I started to hire his services to take me and my SX100 black smoke monitor, to the Warren Springs Laboratory in Stevenage shortly after Bryan's death. The scientists I went to see were impressed with my progress but no more than that, warning me of the new technology coming through.

One morning, I received a call at work from my answering service telling me that a Doctor Bernard van Elzakker was trying to reach me from Holland. Bernard was in charge of the Air Research Laboratory at the Dutch Government RIVM Institute, Netherlands National Institute for Public Health, based in Bilthoven in Holland. He had heard about my SX100, presumably from Warren Springs, and wanted to know a lot more about it. What was this all about? I wondered.

It turned out that RIVM had many "black smoke bubblers" which they wanted to replace with automated machines which could be incorporated into their remotely operated network covering all of the main cities in Holland. They were going to invite manufacturers to submit machines for evaluation and they he wanted to see my SX100.

Currently there were two other candidate machines, one from Holland and one from Germany. Would my SX100 make up a trio? Where was all this going to lead?

Once again I hired Alan Cracknell, this time to take me and my SX100 to Bilthoven to meet Bernard van Elzakker. We were well received and great interest was shown. My willingness to listen to Bernard, he spoke perfect English, and absorb the suggestions he made to bring the machine into line with their requirements, meant that Alan and I would be making many trips to Bilthoven, all at cost to me for the time being, an endeavour which would use up my BT holiday entitlement a few days at a time.

A typical trip from Hereford to Bilthoven involved travelling by car with the goods to Harwich, to catch the 9pm night ferry to Vlissigen on the Hook of Holland arriving at 8am the following morning, then travelling for several hours, or so, to Bilthoven.

It was always a good feeling to arrive at Harwich waiting to board the vessel. It was an even better feeling to get on board, find our cabin and then go to the restaurant where we could eat as much as we liked for £10. Retiring to the lounge for drinks, we were entertained by a "master of ceremonies" calling himself Johnny Walker. This ebullient man, with a red face, dressed in a Union Jack waistcoat, and armed with a radio-microphone, spoke four languages moving effortlessly from one to another as he masterminded party games and music for all of the coach tourists.

Next morning, much the worse for drinking and losing an hour of sleep due to clock adjustments, we would make our way to Bilthoven, to meet Bernard for the day and then go to the De Biltsche Hoek, our pre-booked hotel nearby. Dutch hotels and hotel food are high quality. The rooms were always large, well-appointed with king-size beds and marbled bathrooms. Next day we would find ways of passing the time by visiting places during the course of making our way back to Vlissigen, to catch the night ferry back to England. On one such occasion we made our way to Utrecht, a city of 300,000 inhabitants, intending to stay for a few hours and to have some lunch. Utrecht is on the banks of the river Rhine. When the river moved south, the old river bed was developed into a canal system which curved its way through the old city – a truly pretty area full of small shops and cafes.

Alan and I had a great time exploring the city but when the time began to run out we made our way back to the multi-storey car park only to find that the car was missing. Had it been stolen? Or were we simply confused as to where we had left it? Best part of an hour passed as we searched frantically when, with much relief, there it was. The car was parked where we had left it, no doubt about it, but it seemed to have travelled two floors higher! Even to this day I have a re-occurring nightmare that involves me trying to find my car in a car park containing 500 vehicles.

Eventually I agreed with Bernard that whenever there was an exchange to be made RIVM would send someone to meet the ferry arriving at Vlissigen in the morning and collect, or deliver, the modified SX100 machine meeting Alan when he landed. Alan would then board the same ferry and return to England on the day sailing. This meant that there was no need for me to make the trip each time. On one occasion Alan attracted the attention of the customs men and, when he landed at Harwich, he was directed into a customs vehicle shed and told to get out of the car. Six customs people then proceeded to inspect the car removing panels and wheels looking for drugs or other contraband. They used dogs to sniff around the car and my SX100 which Alan had on board at the time. They then quizzed Alan about the nature of my business and then asked him to make a declaration that he was not moving prohibited goods and sign to that effect. In all, the inspection took two hours at the end of which time Alan was allowed to telephone me and tell me what was going on. My first concern was that the customs people might have dismantled my machine and in so doing might have upset the adjustments and perhaps broken delicate parts. This proved not to be the case however and eventually they let Alan proceed on his journey back to Hereford ignoring the excessive bags and cases of duty-free alcohol in the boot of the car.

During this period I still lived at 52 Barrs Court Road where I had my studio upstairs. This house, built in 1907, had a cellar which had an earth floor which was somewhat damp. I thought I would improve it by lowering the floor to give increased height and putting a concrete base in. I gave the job to David Sherratt and Co, the builders around the corner where I rented my garage. Mr Sherratt had expanded his business from the days of WW11 when he was involved in building airfields around the country.

The floor was lowered and the concrete base duly laid and allowed to dry. A week later it rained and when I next went down the stairs into the cellar I was met by six inches of water trapped by the new concrete floor. Fortunately the guys at work at Madley loaned me a pump and fire hose for a day or two. For long periods I had the hose coming out of the cellar coal-chute and into the pavement gutter to pump the water into the drain. The problem was eventually solved by another specialist company who sunk a pit in the corner of the room and covered it with a grill. In the pit they fitted a pump which turned on automatically when the water table grew under the concrete slab and pumped the excess out into a small drain at ground level on the other side of the wall. It worked and the cellar was perfectly dry from then on. It was suggested that the lowered floor interrupted an underground water soak-away which dispersed rain water from Aylestone hill behind the house.

This was an example of how genuinely helpful my colleagues at the satellite station could be. It was a wonderful place to work and if you were a youngster you could be involved in any of the many activities of the sports and social club. Everything from hang-gliding to football, and you could join the BT team participating in the annual 70 mile Hay-on-Wye to Chepstow charity raft race which takes place on the Wye over three days whatever the weather.

While I developed the SX100 for the RIVM opportunity I also applied myself to the task of designing a battery monitor which I thought might be useful. At the satellite station all of the equipment in the aerial buildings and elsewhere take power from the normal AC mains supply. However, if this should fail, there are massive diesel engine generator sets which start up to supply the site. The problem is that it takes time for the engines to come on line so in the meantime DC power from huge battery banks around the site provide emergency input into the UPS, uninterruptable power system, to be converted to AC mains for the duration providing a continuance of power for the satellite equipment.

The DC power is generated from scores and scores of 12 volt accumulators wired together in series. As any car owner will say, batteries of this type need to be kept in good condition and the terminal voltage checked from time to time. This was another puzzle I set for myself. How to measure each battery, record its terminal voltage and initiate an alarm if the reading is outside programmed limits. The batteries, kept idle for most of the time, must not fail when called upon at a critical moment.

The measuring set I developed used a hundred or so wires and croc-clips reaching out to connect to every battery. I learned to use high-voltage switches and isolated instrumentation amplifiers. The measurement cycles and recordings were handled by a microprocessor with excellent software written by my colleague Nigel Prosser. After some mishaps I got to the point where it worked very well, however, my employers were not interested in it and I didn't bother to exploit it in the market place, a lost opportunity perhaps?

In the spring of 1994 an unexpected opportunity arrived which would set me off on another, more lucrative, course if I made the correct decisions. Because I was 56 years old I qualified for a new voluntary scheme designed to shed older employees like me from the BT payroll. I was among several older men who were being invited to leave on specifically generous terms. In my case I would be given a pension to start immediately and a lump sum of money based upon the number of years served with the company. I already had two private pensions plans which I had stopped paying into at different times and which were not run together. They were not due to be payable until I was 65 years old and they would not be worth much anyway. If I could cash them in now the sum of money released would allow me to buy extra "years" in the BT pension scheme.

Scanning the market place I soon learned that I was not going to get anything like a decent surrender value bearing in mind the sums of money I had paid in to the plans. It was then that I was told that BT had a section which dealt with just this kind of problem for their employees. I gave them all of the defunct pension details and they secured another £2,000 pounds on top of what I thought I could get.

I cashed-in the private pension plans and bought extra pension years in the BT scheme. When this was all calculated out it meant that I could leave BT with an immediate pension of £400 per month and a cash handshake of £10,000. Not bad for five years service and in a few years I had my state pension to look forward to.

So here is the situation. I had a good sum of money which was in addition to my considerable savings, a pension and, above all, I was a free agent once again. I felt really good about myself and my prospects.

Would I now be able to move into manufacturing properly? Designing and making specialist equipment for the market place? With a good deal of creative expertise, hard work and blessings from

Lady Luck, things might move decidedly in my favour. With my SX100 black smoke monitor project in its early months but going well, I felt ready to apply myself for profit again.

Having seen many poorly made pieces of equipment, items which were flung together with what looked like bits of Meccano, being bought by BT from outside contractors to do special one-off tasks, I now considered approaching the London engineers and asking if they would allow me to quote for the supply of such items.

Chapter 8

Company Business

To be successful or not to be successful, that is the question I reckoned I had the answer to. Success means different things to different people and it comes in various degrees. To me it means being independent; owning my own home, owing nothing to the banks, credit card companies, or anyone, and having savings safely deposited and earning interest. To this end I would be happy with a pot of £200,000, if I could attain to it.

However, I judged that it will always be better for me to invest what savings I had in myself, hopefully for a greater return and the pleasure of being self-sufficient, with the knowledge that all decisions, for better or for worse, lie entirely in my own hands. In so doing, for me to be able to spend my time designing products that people actually queued up to purchase, would be an intense thrill. There would be risk and anxiety, sure, but this is what I chose to do, in fact, I wouldn't know how to stop myself.

Angela and I were celebrating on New Year's Eve 1995 at the *Green Man*, a 15th Century coaching house between Hereford and Ross on the B4224. The party was in the assembly room and after dinner, with funny hats, paper bugles, balloons and bunting, everyone ceased dancing and stood in high expectation as the clock approached midnight. The clock struck twelve and Angela whispered in my ear "A Happy and Prosperous New Year darling". Prosperous it was going to be for the foreseeable future but I didn't know it just yet.

At this time the *Green Man* was owned by Arthur Williams and it was many people's dining-out choice. A lot of people will remember the crispy scampi and chips, beef salads, and the steak sandwich all dressed with fresh salad. At the end of the meal, if you wanted, you received a piping hot silver jug of coffee, a smaller jug of cream and a bowl of brown sugar with mints. A memorable eating experience every time.

The *Green Man* was to be the venue for my factory Christmas party for several years.

While I was employed at the satellite station I saw many items of equipment passing through my section which were badly designed and badly built. These were items which the engineers in London had bought to do specific tasks. I was appalled at the poor quality which I categorized as "rubbish". Apart from discussing it with a few of my colleagues I kept quiet about it but I knew that I could produce better equipment given half a chance.

In 1995 one of my first tasks was to tell the BT engineers in London that I was now a free agent and that my company was open for business. Once you have worked for BT you are part of a large family and, if possible, you will always be on the premium list for favours. However, favours are one thing but for me to get an order from BT to produce professional equipment was something else entirely. Engineers build up a relationship with suppliers and prefer to deal with those who understand their technical requirements, come up with the goods on time, and at the correct price, albeit often without due consideration to the quality it seemed to me.

My first opportunity came when I quoted for a dual 8-way splitter in a 2U case and received the order worth £800 – my very first BT order, jubilation and exaltation!

I was still working from my studio and designed the metal-ware using traditional drawings. Steve Clements, who was now working for me full time, had shown me the wisdom of buying a PC and software for producing printed circuit boards. It wasn't long before he persuaded me to buy a plotter so that we could digitize everything. For the production of metal casing parts I used PEP, Precision Engineering Pieces of Tewkesbury, for the painting of the parts in a shade of grey I used Cleftbridge of Ledbury and for silk-screening of the legends onto the panels I used DB Partners in Cheltenham.

My mother and father were living in my flat in Hafod Road which I had bought from them to release equity so that they could continue visiting my brother David in Australia. In the course of my business, whenever I did a round-robin trip in the car to Tewkesbury, Ledbury and Cheltenham, they would come with me for the outing. The circuit became known to us as the "brandy run" because we always stopped at the Aldi store in Cheltenham to pick up supplies of their favourite tipples.

One day, my right-hand man, Steve, told me that he had the opportunity to work with a mate full time on a roofing contract. It meant long hours and he didn't think that he would be able to work for me anymore. This was a blow and sadly we parted but in a few days he called to say that the roofing contract was not all they were led to believe it was going to be. He told me that he would now stay with me for the long term if he could come back to his job. It was certainly OK by me and I saw it as another cog in the machine: one which I could rely on.

So I was manufacturing equipment for BT. Now the London engineers were helping me along with a succession of orders and the guys at Madley, the satellite station, loaned me a *vector network analyser*, an expensive piece of test equipment, for short periods, whenever I needed it.

Meanwhile the RIVM in Holland were testing my SX100 and it would be some time before I would know if my machine would be chosen as the best from the three candidates. With the black smoke monitor in mind I had chosen the trading name of Enviro Techniques Ltd but now, with the production of radio frequency and satellite equipment for BT making headway, I had to think of a more suitable name for the business. I chose ETL Systems, it would do the trick and I advised Companies House accordingly.

In 1996 BT orders were arriving frequently. I had long since given up the factory unit in Peterchurch for it was clear that no-one would want to travel to the unit all the way from Hereford and back every day. Now I needed both people and somewhere to new to work from.

Alan Brookes, my last boss, had left BT under an extension of the same release scheme that I used. He was a time-served BT employee and the amount of service he had with the company meant that his pension was significantly higher than mine. He didn't really need a job but he joined me as an employee on the basis that he could have the freedom to schedule his time as it suited him. This I agreed to. Having Alan on the payroll was a great asset because he understood the equipment being produced and his loose terms of employment helped with the cash-flow.

Our first "factory" turned out to be acquired space at P.K. Engineering on the Rotherwas industrial estate. I negotiated a rent and permission to erect a wooden-walled enclosure at the rear of their premises. The inside of our enclosure was fitted with white kitchen units and we acquired tables and chairs. The situation was not ideal because it was noisy and dusty, not at all conducive to electronic and radio equipment production, but it had to do.

At first both Alan and Steve would work from these premises often wearing ear defenders as protection from the noise.

My next great asset came in the shape of my daughter Michelle. At the time she was working for Mercia Radio Telephones, a successful Hereford company involved in selling and renting radio transceiver equipment and mobile telephones. Michelle looked after the Worcester shop which was formerly a bank complete with strong-room at the back. She was often there on her own which made Angela and me anxious for her safety given the nature of the stock held in the shop. So I enticed her away hoping that I was doing the correct thing because I knew she loved her colleagues and her work.

Michelle picked up the threads of my operation quickly and started to look after the PAYE and other office routines to do with ordering and despatch of our customer's orders.

With our production premises becoming increasingly unsatisfactory I looked for new accommodation. One option was a vacant suite of rooms belonging to another Rotherwas company making low-cost jewellery. Always valuing a consensus of opinion I asked everyone to come with me on my second viewing of the proposed accommodation. When we were shown into the premises again, the hitherto vacant rooms were now filled with camp beds, primus stoves and woks. I declined to take this option further.

We finally found a suitable unit on the Foley Trading Estate in Hereford and moved in at the end of 1996. This unit was 800 sq ft with a mezzanine first floor. Here we stayed, taking over adjacent units as we expanded, during the following years.

The equipment we manufactured was ideally suited to a type of customer new to us. At this time the cable industry consisted of many individual providers which were operating on a city by city basis. They all needed satellite equipment for their head-end as they called it. This is the infrastructure which included the dish aerial and all of the signal distribution equipment which we manufactured. With the barest of sales effort we made contact with all known potential customers and quite soon they were lining up asking for quotations.

Gradually all of the cable companies amalgamated into one or other of two organisations, Telewest and

NTL. Eventually these merged to form Virgin Media as it is today. At the time however, we did very well.

One extraordinary episode involved the CWC at Bromley. We designed and supplied a large amount of equipment to fulfil a perceived role and we were responsible for installation. However, the whole site project was managed by CWC people who kept interfering and changing their minds about all of the equipment requirements and other silly things.

Our guys, having fitted the equipment into the racks would finish a run of cabling only to be told that all of the cable "ties" which fastened them together had to be changed to a different colour. We were on a fixed contract with Steve and Paul Neads on site and they kept making demands upon us. I finally recalled Steve and Paul and told the CWC management that we were backing out of the contract and wanted nothing more to do with it. This meant that I had to get used to the fact that the £40,000 we were owed wouldn't get paid.

I was threatened with a lawsuit but I had made up my mind. After some weeks, I received a telephone call from the team leader of a KPMG management group who had been drafted in to sort out the mess that involved the whole site. I was listened to sympathetically as I answered their questions about our involvement in our part of the project. These men and women were professionals and knew what they wanted. The outcome was that I would be paid the amount owed to us, in full, immediately and I would be commissioned to design a completely new system to meet KPMG team requirements. Many telephone conferences followed but I was happy.

The new equipment was built and installed and it worked perfectly. I heard many years later that our part of the whole site was the only part which was wholly reliable, never gave any trouble and which continued to give good service.

All of the orders we were receiving for equipment of this nature I knew would eventually dry up as the market sector became saturated. But just as these negative thoughts began to invade my mind, I received a call from Bernard at RIVM in Holland to say that the result of the tests showed that my SX100 black smoke monitor had beaten the German rival machine and the home-grown Dutch machine. I was ecstatic. At last the lengthy tests had been completed and my machine was tops, I had beaten the Germans and the Dutch. It was now a matter of costs and prices. Bernard asked me to prepare a price and delivery schedule for 20 machines. I thought I would need £7000 for each one.

After due consideration I telephoned Bernard to say that I wasn't happy with the SX100 and that I would have to design a new machine. He was dismayed at this thought but I pointed out that not only was the SX100 difficult to manufacture and test, it was also difficult to service. I would design a new system which would have interchangeable parts and a fault reporting feature. I would call it the SX200 and I told Bernard not to worry.

Now that RIVM had made their decision, pressure on me was magnified when Walter Trocht from the Belgian government also called to ask for a quotation for six machines. Both the Dutch and the Belgian governments would have to publish their

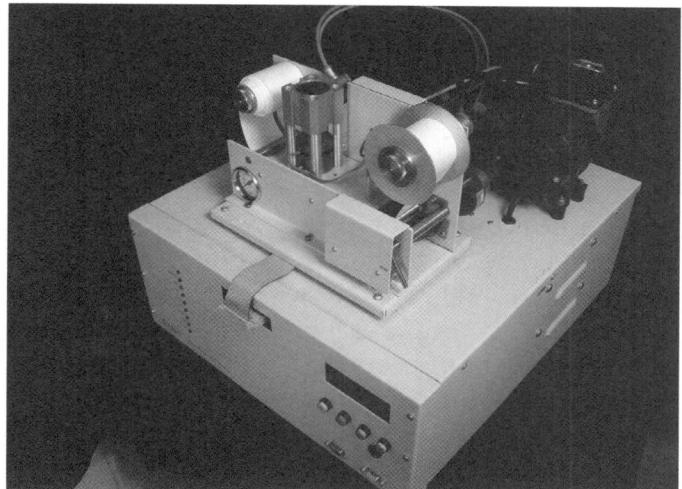

The SX200 Black Particulates Monitor
purchased by the Dutch government.

requirements for new machines to comply with EEC
law on tendering but I was told, with certainty, that
it would only be a formality.

The only way I knew of getting through my day-
to-day work load was to use a large notebook. This
helped me to organise my thoughts and to set my
agenda of things to do, by writing everything down.
It is a well-known fact that this increases efficiency
but it was essential that, with my poor memory, I
didn't forget anything. I would be at a loss if I mislaid
my notebook which provided organised knee-jerk
reactions throughout the day.

At times I found the anxiety and pressure almost
intolerable but a few drinks would always help me
along and, in the summer, early evening walks with
Angela across the fields and scrub-land of Hollybush

near Eastnor Castle, would always sooth away the pressures of the day.

Life at the factory was good. There were seven of us. We all got on well and the orders were always delivered on time. As a bonding exercise I decreed that we would all go to the pub for lunch and drinks on the last Friday of every month. So, at the appointed time, off to the Volunteer in Harold Street we would go and I would be shepherded to the front of the queue as we approached the entrance. The pub served a variety of beers and excellent food which Michelle ordered by phone in advance during the morning. I will always remember the lemon brulée and the great atmosphere which, however, was sometimes interrupted by my mobile telephone on divert from the factory for the duration. The outing was as much about me letting my hair down as the others enjoying themselves.

By this time Michelle had enrolled in the Open University to study for a degree in Humanities, a six year part-time course which she completed in 2003. She ran the main office in the company and made overseas visits to the continent, and further afield to Singapore with an organised trade mission, and then to Las Vegas where we had a stand at the NAB satellite exhibition.

My son Colin was now working for IBM who had bought K3, a Worcester Company and Colin's original employer. His job entailed trouble-shooting software problems associated with main-frame computers in insurance companies, for example. In 2002 he left IBM and attended Oxford University to obtain his Masters in "Environmental Assessments and Management" and then joined Scott Wilson Co,

Environmental Consultants where today he is a Principal Environmental Specialist.

From time to time Peter Kennedy, one of my old bosses who had also taken early release from British Telecom, would come to the factory to see how we were all getting along. Peter had become self employed and would bid for contracts to do satellite front end installation, and commissioning, anywhere in the world. He was full of enthusiasm about the new role he had carved out for himself and he found that there was no shortage of work from BT with others queuing up for his services.

In September 1998 he negotiated a new contract to assist Granger Telecom engineers for one week in Grozny in Chechnya and, as we often did, we ex-BT guys met Peter for a drink at the Victory the night before he was due to leave. We all considered his trip to be risky but Peter shrugged off the danger. We wished him well.

On October 5 the BBC broadcast the news that telecom engineers had been kidnapped in Chechnya and Peter was among them. He was 46 years of age. We were all deeply worried about events but could only hope and pray that he, indeed all of them, would be released, perhaps if a ransom was forthcoming. However, it is British government advice to international companies, and policy, never to pay a ransom to kidnappers and we feared the worst. Some of our jokes at the Victory now returned to haunt us, we couldn't begin to imagine the horrors he was experiencing.

Our deepest fears were realised when it was eventually reported that all of the engineers had been murdered, beheaded by the captors, upon a payment from bin Laden henchmen. Peter's body was recovered and a service held at Holy Trinity Church in Whitecross Road. He was not a close friend but I was deeply shocked, particularly since we had worked together. I will always remember him. It was on the cards that Peter might have joined ETL Systems in a senior role one day, a creative idea which was mooted by several sources. Had he lived, it might have altered the outcome of the company.

The employees at Madley Satellite Station dedicated the massive aerial No2 to his memory and mounted an etched plaque on the side of the aerial building. I attended the unveiling ceremony, which I found deeply moving.

With the prototype SX200 black smoke monitor completed, I engaged Alan Cracknell again to take me and the new machine over to RIVM to see Bernard. When he first saw the new arrangement I think he had mixed feelings. I demonstrated how the front panel could be simply changed over for a new one, how the mechanism could be changed, and how everything on the machine was accessible. He gradually warmed to it and we left leaving the new SX200 with him for more evaluation tests.

Six weeks later the written orders came through from Holland and Belgium more or less at the same time. I had managed to negotiate 30% payable when the order was placed and we received bank drafts totalling £55,000 immediately and the rest payable on presentation of my invoice due after the factory acceptance tests were completed.

SX200 factory acceptance tests. Mike and Michelle,
Dr Bernard van Elzakker, Walter Trocht and
accompanying engineers.

So far so good. I was so busy I was filling up my
notebooks rapidly and frequently took comfort in my
old friend the beer glass when I had difficult
problems to sort out. At no time did I get any
government financial assistance. There were several
schemes around which might have helped but which
for one reason or another I didn't qualify for. One
ridiculous scheme was only available if the project
you needed funds for, hadn't started yet!

There was also a SMART award worth £40,000
which I applied for several times but was rejected.
However, even failed businessmen I knew seemed to
be able to attract these awards effortlessly and I
couldn't help beginning to wonder if it was a case of
"if your face fits". Everything was paid for using my
own savings, and without recourse to the banks, but
no matter, I was investing in myself and the returns
were good. What I now needed was very
professional accountants and I approached Baker

Tilley in Holmer Road, Hereford. They were pleased to take me on and always made time to see me, more often than not explaining things in simple terms, for I didn't understand accountancy, or the tax avoidance options open to me as profits and bank balances built up and up.

Other experts presented me tax-friendly pension schemes for consideration which I never got involved with preferring not to tie up my money but to keep my cash where I could control it, deliberately forsaking the tax allowances, and avoiding inevitable commissions, costs and risk associated with such plans.

Would I now be able to add to our product range? What other gems could I conjure up?

Chapter 9

The Matrix

I rightly deduced that the company needed another product to promote. It would have to be something unique, with good market potential and capable of earning useful revenue. I would have to design a "matrix". Only one company in America and one in Germany made matrices and I decided to be the UK manufacturer for these and add it to our sales portfolio, and become the "third kid on the block", you might say.

This sort of matrix is used by major satellite earth stations to switch incoming signals from the many dish aerials on site, through to a myriad of receivers.

Without any experience other than an appreciation of lower microwave principles, learned by doing, I set about the task of producing a prototype.

I chose to design a unit which would have 32 inputs and 32 outputs. Any input must be able to be switched to one or more outputs making the transitions electronically. It would be bulky since it would contain 64 large printed circuit boards, 32 mounted vertically which would be directly plugged in to 32 mounted horizontally.

The number of intersections, or cross points, would be 1024. All these interconnections would

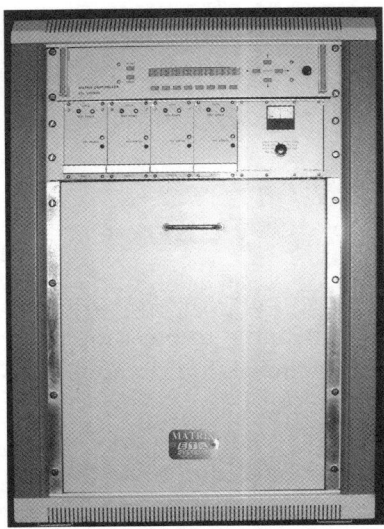

Original 32x32 L-band matrix complete with control unit and dual power supply.

require a plug and socket which had to have low mechanical insertion force and to be of sufficient quality to be able to work at microwave frequencies. On top of this, because there were so many, 2048 in total, they had to be low-cost.

Meeting all of the problems head-on we designed our own plug and socket and found that we could get really good prices for precision gold-plated parts from factories in Taiwan. Fortunately, the days when you had to order 100,000 pieces were over and it was now possible to order only a few thousand which made our matrix project viable.

Since the individual large circuit boards, each carrying 32 connectors had to be able to be unplugged for servicing, the next worry was how to pre-locate everything so that this process could be carried out easily. Using nothing more than an intermediate metal plate with precision punched holes as a guide for the connectors, we found that once the 64 boards were all mechanically locked together, sufficient mass existed for an individual board to be removed safely.

By now the company had purchased its own sophisticated test equipment, expensive Vector Network Analysers from Hewlett Packard at £3000 each. I remember watching the screen of one of these as Steve Clements turned on the power and began to electronically step through each matrix interconnection to check its performance for the first time. There were 1024 tests to be made but by the time we reached test 20, I could already see that we had a winner and I proclaimed with pride "we have a new product!" to the rest of the factory team gathered round expectantly.

On the strength of our success I provided a quote for Sky Television and calculated that £30,000 each was the best price to charge and even before the prototype was fully tested we had a firm order.

You can never be too careful about trumpeting success to people. I had a visit to the factory by the managing director of another local company, a man I respected very much. I was thrilled at the success I was having with the matrix and thrilled to tell him all about it, even that I had a quotation with Sky in the pipe-line. A few days later, to my horror, my Sky customer rang to tell me that they had had a quote from this man. I had trusted him and thought we were on friendly terms with each other but nothing could have been further from the truth.

In 2001 the company was manufacturing a wide range of equipment and shipping a good proportion of it overseas. I was for ever striving to find quality parts to buy at competitive prices and started to look to Asia for solutions.

To get cheaper printed circuit boards I sent an engineer to China, to a factory in Guangdong province we had contact with, to set up the process. The idea was to buy fully assembled boards many of which had tiny transformer coils fitted. It turned out that we could buy these boards fully assembled and tested for only £1 each, a saving of £30 if manufactured here!

When my engineer returned, he described how the Chinese were manufacturing their products sat cross-legged on the floor of their factory unit. Western style food was difficult to find and pigeon was a popular choice on the menu. Apparently the pigeon was served up, beak, head, feathers and all, having been cooked whole in boiling fat. I suggested to my staff that perhaps we could do this and ask for pigeon for lunch at the Volunteer. It would be cheaper, but I was met by incredulous stares.

In June 2001, I got to know a very stylish lady of the sea. She was the P&O ship Aurora, a sleek beauty of 76,000 tons. Angela and I had booked a two-week cruise in the Mediterranean visiting Malaga, Nice, Naples, Venice, Dubrovnik and Gibraltar. I was 63 years old and needed this holiday for I was beginning to feel the strain of running this lively business of mine.

The Aurora, so called after the Roman goddess of sunrise, had entered service in April 2000. She was built at the Meyer Werft yard in Germany at a cost of 375 million dollars. Having ten decks she can carry a total of 1875 passengers, in style and comfort, and has a crew complement of 850. We found this gleaming white ship with highly varnished woodwork and handrails a breathtaking sight to see when we arrived at Southampton, her home port, on embarkation day.

I was tired and this holiday did me the power of good. Nevertheless, work was ever on my mind and I wondered how long I could keep up the pace. To step back a little from it, I started to arrive later for work at 9am. The staff preferred to start early and finish early which was OK by me.

September the 11 2001 was just one such morning. When I walked in, I was told about the first attack on the World Trade Centre in New York by one of the staff. Shortly afterwards the second tower was hit and within two hours both had collapsed with the loss of nearly 3000 civilian lives.

There are only five catastrophes which have had a lasting effect on me, which immediately come vividly to my mind and this was one of them, the other four being the assassination of John F. Kennedy in November 1963, the Aberfan disaster in October 1966, The Princess of Wales death in August 1997 and hearing of Peter Kennedy's abduction. I will always remember where I was on each occasion

In 2001 we moved from Barrs Court Road to a four-bedroomed house in Bodenham Road set back on sloping ground. I contracted Brian Marsden to landscape the front of the house and to create a brick-covered driveway. I had the whole house decorated, a new fire place installed and new carpets laid. There was space in the downstairs toilet for a glass-fronted corner shower unit which I had installed the same time that the upstairs bathroom fittings were changed. This work was carried out to perfection by Westdown Bathrooms.

Shortly afterwards whether through earthquake or by alterations at the front of the house we noticed that the walls were beginning to crack. Hereford is on an earthquake fault line and there were tremors at that time. Sensing trouble I engaged a professional building engineer to survey the property. The downstairs carpets had to be lifted and several inspection holes drilled through the floor to test the sub-structure. Apparently this 1970's house had been built in the old way with the walls, and thus the weight of the house, rested on the concrete floor slab or raft. Nowadays the walls are built resting on footings with the floor laid afterwards.

Tests revealed that there were large voids under the concrete floor where there should have been infill. As a matter of urgency, a multitude of four inch holes had to be drilled all across the downstairs floor and then ten tons of liquid concrete poured in to stabilize it from underneath.

Angela was in despair for there was dust and thick, dirty, plastic sheeting everywhere leaving us no choice but to live upstairs for ten days with excursions to the kitchen. Fortunately the large lorry containing the mixing and pumping machinery could draw up alongside the house by using the wide driveway belonging to the retirement home next door. Several hoses brought the liquid grout from the mixer to the various holes.

When the engineers had left we set about clearing up the mess and redecorating again. The remedy had cost me £10,000 which I was unable to claim from my insurance company.

In July 2001 my dad died. Arthur was 94 years of age and had been failing for the past few months. The cremation was a private occasion but because he was well known in the city I organised a memorial service at St Peter's church and advertised it in the Hereford Times not knowing if many, if any, would turn up. On the day the church was almost full and I was delighted.

Mid 2002 I was feeling tired, I was 64 years old and I started to think about retirement and the prospect of selling the company. I desperately wanted it to end up in the hands of someone who appreciated the potential of the business, someone who would take it to the next level and make it truly international.

I engaged a Worcester agency to find buyers and, in due course, they provided a list of possible candidates. There were people with money who were interested but none of them understood the technical aspects of the business and consequently were never likely to make a success of it or pay the sale price I wanted.

Then, I was introduced to the two partners, Ian Hilditch a business graduate and Dr Esen Bayar a chartered engineer, who were just perfect with all of the right credentials I had hoped for. I knew in my heart that these two would see the business move forward.

These men were keen, even so, I could not bring myself to believe that if I proceeded I would lose everything I have worked for, just for money. I spent long periods in personal denial agonising over a final decision.

You will already know the outcome.

Today ETL Systems Ltd employs 46 people engaged in design and manufacturing microwave

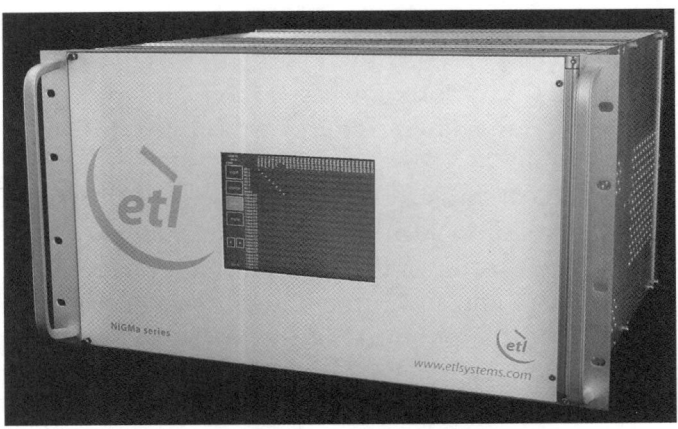

The latest compact and powerful Nigma-series matrix
from ETL Systems.

components and systems. They have a new building
on the site of the Coldwell Radio Station, near the
satellite station at Madley. The original radio station
was used to send high quality TV signals from the
satellite station to London and the site came on the
market for sale when radio transmission gave way
to superior fibre optic links and the building became
redundant.

The company still manufactures a matrix but
now there are many types, some small and compact,
and many mammoth-size systems in countries all
over the world with customers ranging from
commercial to military. As you would expect, The
Queens Award to Enterprise, and The Queens Award
for International Trade, has been won many times
and I am immensely proud.